INTRODUCING
ISSUES WITH
OPPOSING
VIEWPOINTS®

Athletes and Drug Use

Jennifer L. Skancke and Lauri S. Friedman, *Book Editors*

GREENHAVEN PRESS
A part of Gale, Cengage Learning

GALE
CENGAGE Learning™

Detroit • New York • San Francisco • New Haven, Conn • Waterville, Maine • London

Christine Nasso, *Publisher*
Elizabeth Des Chenes, *Managing Editor*

For more information, contact:
Greenhaven Press
27500 Drake Rd.
Farmington Hills, MI 48331-3535
Or you can visit our Internet site at gale.cengage.com

For product information and technology assistance, contact us at

Gale Customer Support, 1-800-877-4253
For permission to use material from this text or product, submit all requests online at
www.cengage.com/permissions

Further permissions questions can be emailed to permissionrequest@cengage.com

LIBRARY OF CONGRESS CATALOGING-IN-PUBLICATION DATA

Athletes and drug use / Jennifer L. Skancke and Lauri S. Friedman, book editors.
   p. cm. — (Introducing issues with opposing viewpoints)
 Includes bibliographical references and index.
 ISBN 978-0-7377-4166-7 (hardcover)
1. Doping in sports. 2. Athletes—Drug use. 3. Anabolic steroids—Health aspects. I.
Friedman, Lauri S. II. Skancke, Jennifer.
  RC1230.A86 2009
  362.29—dc22

                                      2008028525

Printed in the United States of America
1 2 3 4 5 6 7 12 11 10 09 08

Contents

Chapter 3: How Can Drug Use Among Student Athletes Be Curbed?

Foreword

Indulging in a wide spectrum of ideas, beliefs, and perspectives is a critical cornerstone of democracy. After all, it is often debates over differences of opinion, such as whether to legalize abortion, how to treat prisoners, or when to enact the death penalty, that shape our society and drive it forward. Such diversity of thought is frequently regarded as the hallmark of a healthy and civilized culture. As the Reverend Clifford Schutjer of the First Congregational Church in Mansfield, Ohio, declared in a 2001 sermon, "Surrounding oneself with only like-minded people, restricting what we listen to or read only to what we find agreeable is irresponsible. Refusing to entertain doubts once we make up our minds is a subtle but deadly form of arrogance." With this advice in mind, Introducing Issues with Opposing Viewpoints books aim to open readers' minds to the critically divergent views that comprise our world's most important debates.

Introducing Issues with Opposing Viewpoints simplifies for students the enormous and often overwhelming mass of material now available via print and electronic media. Collected in every volume is an array of opinions that captures the essence of a particular controversy or topic. Introducing Issues with Opposing Viewpoints books embody the spirit of nineteenth-century journalist Charles A. Dana's axiom: "Fight for your opinions, but do not believe that they contain the whole truth, or the only truth." Absorbing such contrasting opinions teaches students to analyze the strength of an argument and compare it to its opposition. From this process readers can inform and strengthen their own opinions, or be exposed to new information that will change their minds. Introducing Issues with Opposing Viewpoints is a mosaic of different voices. The authors are statesmen, pundits, academics, journalists, corporations, and ordinary people who have felt compelled to share their experiences and ideas in a public forum. Their words have been collected from newspapers, journals, books, speeches, interviews, and the Internet, the fastest growing body of opinionated material in the world.

Introducing Issues with Opposing Viewpoints shares many of the well-known features of its critically acclaimed parent series, Opposing Viewpoints. The articles are presented in a pro/con format, allowing readers to absorb divergent perspectives side by side. Active reading questions preface each viewpoint, requiring the student to approach the material thoughtfully and carefully. Useful charts, graphs, and cartoons supplement each article. A thorough introduction provides readers with crucial background on an issue. An annotated bibliography points the reader toward articles, books, and Web sites that contain additional information on the topic. An appendix of organizations to contact contains a wide variety of charities, nonprofit organizations, political groups, and private enterprises that each hold a position on the issue at hand. Finally, a comprehensive index allows readers to locate content quickly and efficiently.

Introducing Issues with Opposing Viewpoints is also significantly different from Opposing Viewpoints. As the series title implies, its presentation will help introduce students to the concept of opposing viewpoints and learn to use this material to aid in critical writing and debate. The series' four-color, accessible format makes the books attractive and inviting to readers of all levels. In addition, each viewpoint has been carefully edited to maximize a reader's understanding of the content. Short but thorough viewpoints capture the essence of an argument. A substantial, thought-provoking essay question placed at the end of each viewpoint asks the student to further investigate the issues raised in the viewpoint, compare and contrast two authors' arguments, or consider how one might go about forming an opinion on the topic at hand. Each viewpoint contains sidebars that include at-a-glance information and handy statistics. A Facts About section located in the back of the book further supplies students with relevant facts and figures.

Following in the tradition of the Opposing Viewpoints series, Greenhaven Press continues to provide readers with invaluable exposure to the controversial issues that shape our world. As John Stuart Mill once wrote: "The only way in which a human being can make some approach to knowing the whole of a subject is by hearing what can be said about it by persons of every variety of opinion and studying all modes in which it can be looked at by every character of mind. No wise man ever acquired his wisdom in any mode but this." It is to this principle that Introducing Issues with Opposing Viewpoints books are dedicated.

Introduction

Performance-enhancing drug use is often associated with sports that are largely the dominion of male athletes, such as baseball, football, and professional wrestling. However, female athletes are also using these substances in increasing numbers, sometimes at higher rates than their male counterparts. While the drug use of female athletes may not get much attention except for the occasional Olympic scandal, it does suggest that efforts to reduce steroid use among teenagers must focus on both boys and girls.

Performance-enhancing drug use among young women exists at the high school and college level. In 2004 the Centers for Disease Control (CDC) released a survey of U.S. high school students that showed that 5.3 percent of girls between the ages of fourteen and seventeen had taken steroids without a legal prescription, compared to 6.8 percent of boys. In addition, a study released by the National Collegiate Athletic Association (NCAA) in 2006 found that in 2005, although steroid use was in decline among female athletes, they were using the stimulants amphetamines and ephedrine in increasing quantities. For example, 5.2 percent of women softball players and 4.4 percent of women swimmers reported using amphetamines. Furthermore, while male tennis players used amphetamines at a higher rate than their female counterparts (3.9 percent to 2.6 percent), women basketball players took amphetamines and ephedrine more frequently than male participants did (2.9 percent versus 1.2 percent for amphetamines and 1.5 percent versus 1 percent for ephedrine). Clearly, the use of performance-enhancing drugs by female athletes is quickly catching up to, and in some cases surpassing, drug use by male athletes.

Female athletes use performance-enhancing drugs for different reasons than their male peers. Linn Goldberg, an expert on student drug use, is the director of the ATLAS (Athletes Training and Learning to Avoid Steroids) and ATHENA (Athletes Targeting Healthy Exercise and Nutrition Alternatives) antidrug programs. As Goldberg explained in a 2007 interview, "Generally, we found that boys are trying to get as large as possible while girls want to be smaller for both appearance reasons and to help them move faster."[1] As a result, male athletes tend to use steroids to help them increase strength and body mass, but female athletes typically shy away from this particular class of performance-enhancing drug because they want to avoid side effects such as facial hair growth and the cessation of menstruation. For women who have used steroids, the consequences can be devastating—in April 1987 East German heptathlete Birgit Dressel died at the age of twenty-six as a result of steroid use. Cancer and heart diseases have also afflicted former female steroid users. Although they have lower rates of steroid use, female athletes appear to be more likely to use amphetamines—such as those found in diet pills—because they think it will help them lose weight and increase reaction time.

Although they may use performance-enhancing drugs for different reasons than male athletes do, these girls and women also want to compete at the highest level, and they may feel pressure to take drugs that will help them achieve this goal. Such pressure is what prompted sprinter Kelli White to take the steroid THG. As she explained in testimony before Congress, she took the drug in 2003 at the suggestion of her advisers. She states, "I began using these substances not to give me an advantage, but because I had become convinced I needed to use them to level the playing field with my competitors. It is a very troubling situation when you have trained to compete in a sport at the highest level, but feel those with which you are competing have an unfair advantage."[2] While using steroids helped make her the fastest woman in the world, winning the 2003 U.S. and world titles in the 100- and 200-meter races, they also caused side effects such as severe acne and high blood pressure and had legal consequences: White was banned from her sport for two years for her actions. A similar fate befell her fellow U.S. Olympian Marion Jones, who was stripped of the medals she had won at the 2000 Olympics after admitting she took steroids. Jones was also sentenced to jail for six months for lying to federal investigators.

Keeping young women from using performance-enhancing drugs requires them to be educated about the dangerous effects of these substances. To this end, the ATHENA program teaches teenage girls not only about the physical effects of steroids but also about developing healthy exercise and nutrition habits. Studies show that girls who participate in ATHENA are three times less likely to use diet pills and half as likely to use steroids or amphetamines. These efforts were so significant, they were noted by the Government Accountability

Office (GAO), which investigates issues for Congress. As the GAO found in November 2007, "Girls who participated in the program reported less ongoing and new abuse of anabolic steroids as well as a reduction in the abuse of other performance-enhancing and body-shaping substances."[3]

Although performance-enhancing drug use is a newer problem in female competitors, drug use among athletes is an issue that affects both genders at all levels, ages, and kinds of sport. In *Introducing Issues with Opposing Viewpoints: Athletes and Drug Use*, authors debate issues such as the ethics of performance-enhancing drug use, the appropriate consequences for athletes who use those drugs, and the best way to reduce their use among teenage athletes.

Notes

1. Linn Goldberg, interview, "SOM Programs Targeting Teen Athletes Garner NFL, *Sports Illustrated* Support," Oregon Health and Science University, October 26, 2007. www.ohsu.edu/ohsuedu/academic/som/dean/community-spotlight-atlas.cfm.
2. Kelli White, statement hearing before the Committee on Commerce, Science, and Transportation, United States Senate, 109th Cong. 1st sess., May 24, 2005, p. 14. http://bulk.resource.org/gpo.gov/hearings/109s/24722.txt.
3. U.S. Government Accountability Office (GAO), "Anabolic Steroid Abuse: Federal Efforts to Prevent and Reduce Anabolic Steroid Use Among Teenagers," GAO-08-15, November 30, 2007. www.gao.gov/htext/d0815.html.

Chapter 1

Should Drug Use Among Athletes Be Illegal?

Performance-enhancing drugs are used by some athletes, such as 1988 100-meter dash gold medalist Ben Johnson, to increase their speed, strength, and endurance during athletic competition.

Performance-Enhancing Drugs Should Be Illegal

Marissa Saltzman

"Most athletes and fans agree that performance-enhancement drugs should not have a place in sports."

In the following viewpoint Marissa Saltzman argues that performance-enhancing drugs should be illegal. Performance-enhancing drugs are used by some athletes to increase their speed, strength, and endurance during athletic competition. Although these substances are banned in some sports, not a single unifying regulation has made performance-enhancing drug use illegal across the board. She complains that these illegal stimulants should not be allowed because they give athletes an unfair advantage. In fact, some sports have been lax to punish athletes who test positive for these substances. Saltzman concludes that all serious competitions need to test athletes and disqualify any person who violates the ban on performance-enhancing drugs.

Saltzman wrote this article for *Odyssey*, a youth science magazine, while a junior at Mount Holyoke College in Massachusetts.

AS YOU READ, CONSIDER THE FOLLOWING QUESTIONS:

1. What punishment did American sprinter Kelli White receive for violating the ban on performance-enhancing drugs, according to the author?
2. According to the author, what harmful effects do steroids have on the human body?
3. In what way can steroids be psychologically addicting, according to the author?

It's May 2004. American sprinter Kelli White, 27, has just lost every medal she won during the past four years. She has also lost her chance to compete in the 2004 Athens Olympics.

The athlete's use of the stimulant Modafinil, a prescription drug, as well as evidence that she used erthropoietin, an endurance-enhancing hormone, ultimately led to her downfall. In a statement issued by her attorney, White laments, "In doing this, I have not only cheated myself, but also my family, friends, and sport."

According to news accounts, White was first introduced to performance-enhancing drugs in 2000 through a contact of her childhood coach. Initially, she didn't realize that the "flaxseed oil" he provided was actually a designer steroid. When she discovered this, she immediately stopped taking it. But in 2003, she returned to her drug source, determined to gain an added edge through any means available.

Within two weeks of starting multiple performance-enhancing drugs, she noticed a difference. "You could run harder, longer," she told the press. But along with her developing muscles and shortened sprint times, White also acquired a raspy voice and acne. She couldn't stand looking at her picture on TV. "I felt that to do this [drug use], I had to become someone totally different than I was," she revealed to the world. "I look at that person and I'm like, 'That's not Kelli White. That's not who I am, who I started out to be.'"

Athletes in all fields are under extreme pressure. In addition to their own drive for success, they are pressured by coaches, family, and fans. Dr. Cynthia M. Kuhn, professor of pharmacology at Duke University, explains why the pressure continues to escalate. "The higher you go, the more pressure there is to win, and the greater the pressure is to win at any cost," she says. For some, no method is too risky.

That Extra Edge

A performance-enhancement drug is any substance that is taken for the sole purpose of enhancing athletic performance. The practice is often referred to as "doping" and can cause serious medical problems. Doping is most prevalent among professional athletes. However, officials in all sports are implementing more rigorous drug testing of participants and banning any athlete who fails.

And there are many who do. Tennis player Mariano Puerta, a finalist in the French Open, was penalized in December 2005 for

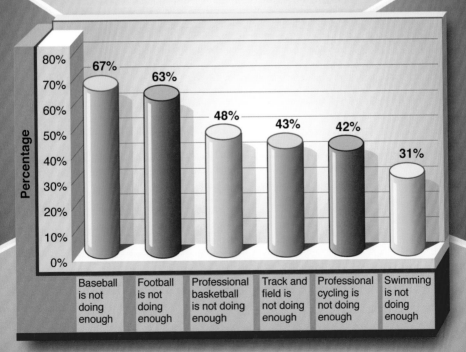

Sports Fans Want Illegal Drug Use Curbed

Almost two of out of three sports fans say baseball and football need to do more to curb illegal drug use in their sports. Almost half of all basketball, track and field, and professional cycling fans say the same.

Taken from: *USA Today*/Gallup poll, 2007.

his second doping violation—this time, he was suspended for eight years, essentially the rest of his professional career. In January 2006, Bulgarian teenager Sesil Karatantcheva became the second woman tennis player to receive a ban as a result of a drug offense.

There are many different kinds of performance-enhancement drugs: some prescription, some over the counter, and others, illegal. Depending on the drug type, they help athletes to relax, work through pain and fatigue, build mass and muscle, hide other drug use, or increase oxygen supply to the exercising body tissues. Sounds good, but the downside is often hidden.

While legal substances such as high-protein drinks, caffeine, and nutritional supplements appeal to some athletes, for others they just aren't enough. These athletes turn to stronger drugs that promise greater results, as well as carry more serious risks. One category of enhancement drug that has received increased attention over the past decade is anabolic steroids. Sports relying on upper body mass and endurance, such as weightlifting, swimming, football, and gymnastics, are more likely to foster steroid-using athletes than those that rely more on dexterity and coordination.

FAST FACT

According to a December 2007 MSN-Zogby poll, 85 percent of American sports fans believe that sports leagues and governing bodies should take any steps necessary to eliminate the use of performance-enhancing drugs in sports.

The "Juice"

Known as "roids," "juice," "hype," "pump," or "gym candy," steroids are man-made chemicals similar to the male hormone testosterone. Steroids trick the body into believing that testosterone, which aids in muscle development, is being produced. Anabolic steroids can be taken as either pills or injections. While doctors may legally prescribe them to treat some medical conditions, anabolic steroids have become increasingly abused by athletes who are desperate to gain a fine margin of edge. After all, in professional athletics, everyone is a great athlete, but someone has to be the best. . . .

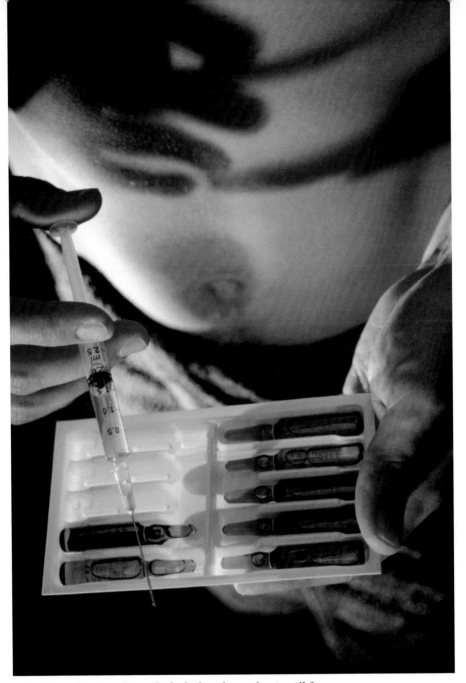

Steroids can be injected into the body directly or taken in pill form.

Changing the protein synthesis in muscle tissue has both positive and negative effects. While it can increase an athlete's ability to handle workloads (kick a field goal; lift a massive weight), it can also result in excess production of cholesterol, a substance that has been linked to heart disease. Prolonged use of these steroids can damage vital organs such as the liver, heart, and kidneys. Steroids and other performance-enhancing drugs are especially damaging to adolescents whose bodies are still developing, because they halt bone growth prematurely.

When steroids reach the brain, they affect the hypothalamus and the limbic system. The hypothalamus controls the body's hormone levels. Steroids can lower testosterone in males and disrupt menstrual cycles in females. The limbic system, which controls our emotions, can also be altered by steroids, resulting in changes in mood and memory. According to Dr. Harrison G. Pope, Jr., director of the Biological Psychiatry Laboratory at McLean Hospital in Belmont, MA, the mental side effects can range from irritability to aggressiveness to even some cases of violence. While some users experience no mood changes, Pope explains, "it's a biochemical idiosyncrasy, and you can't tell in advance which group you'd be in." . . .

Information, steroids can remain in your body from one week to three or four months. These drugs can also be addicting, both on the physical level as well as on the psychological level. Dr. David L. Katz, director of the Prevention Research Center at Yale University School of Medicine and associate professor of public health, explains why: "An elite female athlete is caught using steroids, and the implication is that steroid use contributed to the elite performance," he says. "This creates an enormous pressure for ambitious athletes to use such drugs, or run the risk that they will lose to opponents who do."

As the Olympic Games and other serious competitions are becoming more closely monitored to prevent steroid-using athletes from competing, some researchers are optimistic that this will decrease steroid use. "As it becomes unacceptable for elite athletes and for professional athletes [to use performance-enhancement drugs], I think that the allure will decrease," says Kuhn. "I'm optimistic that use will decrease as coaches learn that [the drugs] don't help, and actually could harm their athletes."

Either way, doctors, drug researchers, sports officials, and most athletes and fans agree that performance-enhancement drugs should not have a place in sports. "Any use of dangerous drugs to alter the bounds of human performance is too much use," says Katz. "The bounds of human performance should be a measure of will and dedication, not the effects of pharmacology."

Adam Schlauch, 13, a competitor in the 2005 Cyclocross National Championships, agrees: "If you just work hard at it, you can accomplish anything."

EVALUATING THE AUTHOR'S ARGUMENTS:

Marissa Saltzman quotes from several sources to support the points she makes in her essay. Make a list of everyone she quotes, including their credentials and the nature of their comments. Then, analyze her sources—are they credible? Are they well qualified to speak on the subject?

Viewpoint

2

Performance-Enhancing Drugs Should Be Legal

Adrianne Blue

"Sport's dirty little secret is drugs, and it is high time we made them legal."

In the following viewpoint Adrianne Blue argues in favor of legalizing performance-enhancing drugs. Blue claims that most top-level athletes use performance-enhancing drugs to build muscle, speed, and endurance. However, when performance-enhancing drugs are banned from sports competition, it does not necessarily reduce their use among athletes. Instead, the ban forces athletes to take drugs underground, where they are consumed in secret. The consequence of this, Blue argues, is that the drugs are not regulated by physiotherapists and doctors who know how to best manage them. Athletes become at risk for overdosing or doing irreparable physical damage. Blue concludes that legalizing performance-enhancing drugs can protect athletes from dangerously abusing them.

Blue is a writer, broadcaster, and a senior lecturer in international journalism at London's City University. Previously she was the deputy sports editor and literary editor at *Time Out,* a magazine devoted to events and culture in the world's largest cities.

AS YOU READ, CONSIDER THE FOLLOWING QUESTIONS:
1. According to the author, why do athletes take performance-enhancing drugs?
2. What does the author mean when she says that sports doping does not give athletes a "free ride?"
3. How would legalizing performance-enhancing drugs protect amateur athletes on the rise, according to the author?

The dirty little secret in sport used to be money. Champions were turned into criminals, forced to queue up for illegal cash payments handed out in brown envelopes. Why? Because top-level sport was a full-time profession—you could not hope to achieve world class by training after hours—but sports champions were supposed to be amateurs. Today, sport's dirty little secret is drugs, and it is high time we made them legal. Performance-enhancing drugs may not be desirable, but they are here to stay. What we can do away with is the hypocrisy.

Most Top Athletes Use Performance-Enhancing Drugs

Insiders know that many—perhaps most—top players in all sports take drugs to train harder and feel no pain during play. The trainers, sports doctors, nutritionists, physiotherapists and managers of the big names make sure banned substances are taken at the safest and most efficient levels, and when they can, the governing bodies look the other way.

The fastest man on the planet and the world's top endurance athlete have just failed drug tests. The runner Justin Gatlin, the current [2006] Olympic 100 meter champion and co-holder of the world record, and the cyclist Floyd Landis, winner of this year's [2006] Tour de France, are getting some bad publicity, but they are in very good company. Cricket, football, tennis and speed skating have all had scandals involving anabolic steroids, growth hormones,

FAST FACT

Under U.S. law, trafficking in steroids can result in a five-year prison sentence.

A Timeline of Drug Use in Sports

Athletes have looked to drugs to gain a competitive edge since the early twentieth century. Though the issue of drug use in sports became a hot topic in 2005, it was only the latest example of authorities' attempts to crack down on the use of performance-enhancing drugs in sports.

1904
- To keep him going, American Olympic marathon winner Thomas Hicks (USA) is given strychnine and brandy during the race.

1935
- Scientists synthesize testosterone.

1960
- Danish cyclist Knud Enemark Jensen suffers a fatal crash during the road race at the Rome Olympics after taking a stimulant.

1967
- British cyclist Tom Simpson collapses and dies from amphetamine use while ascending Mont Ventoux in the Tour de France. His death spurs the Tour de France to institute doping controls.

1972
- The International Olympic Committee (IOC) begins full-scale drug testing in the Olympics.

1976
- The IOC adds anabolic steroids to its banned list.

1988
- Canadian sprinter Ben Johnson tests positive for an anabolic steroid after winning the 100-meter in world-record time (9.79 seconds). He is stripped of his medal and banned for two years.

1990
- The National Football League institutes a year-round, random steroid testing program.

1993
- The Association of Tennis Professionals, the Women's Tennis Association, and the International Tennis Federation create an anti-doping program.

1998
- Irish swimmer Michelle Smith, who won three gold medals in the 1996 Olympics, is banned for four years for manipulating a urine sample.
- St. Louis Cardinals slugger Mark McGwire admits using androstenedione.

1999
- The National Basketball Association adds steroids to its list of banned substances.

2000
- The World Anti-Doping Agency (WADA) begins operations.
- China cuts twenty-seven athletes and thirteen coaches from its team for the Sydney Olympics, saying some athletes had suspicious test results.
- The IOC implements performance-enhancing drug tests in the Sydney Olympics.
- The U.S. Anti-Doping Agency (USADA) begins operations.

2003–2004
- Government agents raid the Bay Area Laboratory Co-Operative (BALCO). Attorney General John Ashcroft announces a forty-two-count indictment against BALCO founder Victor Conte, BALCO executive James Valente, track coach Remi Korchemny, and trainer Greg Anderson. Among the charges: conspiracy to distribute and possess with intent to distribute anabolic steroids, conspiracy to defraud through misbranded drugs, and money laundering.

2004 • Major League Baseball (MLB) begins mandatory steroid testing for players.

• A record twenty-four athletes are ousted for drug-related violations in the Athens Olympics.

• New York Yankees slugger Jason Giambi and San Francisco Giants star Barry Bonds testify about performance-enhancing drugs. Giambi states he knew he was taking them; Bonds says he did not know.

2005 • Baseball agrees to a new policy banning steroids, masking agents, and diuretics. There will be one unannounced mandatory test of each player during the season. In addition, there will be testing of randomly selected players, with no maximum number, and there wll be random testing during the off-season. The penalties for a positive result are, first positive, 10 days; second, 30 days; third, 60 days; fourth, one year, and all without pay.

• Slugger Jose Canseco admits to taking steroids and accuses many MLB stars of using performance-enhancing drugs in his book, *Juiced: Wild Times, Rampant 'Roids, Smash Hits and How Baseball Got Big.*

• The National Hockey League institutes a drug-testing policy for performance-enhancing substances. Players are tested twice a year. The first positive results in a twenty-game suspension, the second brings sixty games, and the third a permanent ban, though players can apply for reinstatement after two years.

• Rafael Palmeiro of the Baltimore Orioles is given a ten-day suspension for violating MLB's steroid policy. The next day Seattle Mariners pitcher Ryan Franklin is suspended for the same infraction.

• MLB approves a new steroid policy. The penalties for a positive result are now 50 games for a first offense and 100 for a second offense. A third positive test would result in a lifetime ban. It will also test for amphetamines. A first positive test would lead to mandatory additional testing, a second offense would draw a 25-game suspension, and a third offense would get 80 games.

2006 • After winning the Tour de France, U.S. cyclist Floyd Landis tests positive for an illegal testosterone ratio.

• U.S. sprinter Justin Gatlin accepts a positive drug test and a USADA suspension for up to eight years with an option to challenge the finding in arbitration.

2007 • The NFL and its players' union announce changes to toughen its steroid policy, including adding EPO to its list of banned substances, making players suspended for using performance-enhancing drugs forfeit a prorated portion of their signing bonus, increasing from seven to ten the number of players on each team randomly tested each week during the season, and subjecting all players to random carbon isotope ratio testing.

Taken from: Joan Murphy, "Timeline: A Century of Drugs and the Athlete," *USA Today*, March 1, 2007.

Justin Gatlin, who broke the world record for the 100-meter run, was one of many athletes who have failed drug tests.

blood doping, diuretics, amphetamines, or, like Gatlin and Landis, testosterone boosts. You name it, someone takes it if it will help.

"Drugs Allow You to Train Harder"

What many of us don't realize is that sports doping rarely gives you a free ride. If you or I were to take anabolic steroids and sit down in front of the telly [television], we would not build muscle or speed or endurance. Drugs allow you to train harder. They help you recover more quickly from a hard session so you can work hard again the next day. Some drugs boost the body's propensity for building muscle or its ability to use oxygen, but you still have to do the work. A judo medalist once told me, "I took drugs so I could train twice a day. I don't feel any guilt because I know I earned my medal."

This season, the British 100 meters runner Dwain Chambers, who was stripped of his 2002 European Championship title, is back on the team after a two-year ban for taking a designer steroid. The man who welcomed him back, the performance director of UK Athletics,

Dave Collins, said: "We are not making ethical statements. We are picking a team to do as well as we can."

Performance-Enhancing Techniques Have Always Been Used by Athletes

Tales of sport doping go back to ancient Egypt, where the hoof of an Abyssinian ass ground up and boiled in oil was prescribed to improve performance. In the 19th century, boxers took heroin before going into the ring. The legendary 1960s Manchester United goalkeeper Harry Gregg has confessed that he took amphetamines before matches.

No one much cared until 1960, when a Danish cyclist on speed died during an Olympic competition. None the less, it was seven years before the Olympic authorities issued a banned-drug list. Anabolic steroids were not prohibited until 1976. Champions and the testers have been playing cat and mouse ever since.

Legalizing Performance-Enhancing Drugs Will Perfect Athletes

The main effect of banning such substances has been to turn performers and their coaches into liars and cheats. We should legalize performance-enhancing drugs so that they can be regulated and athletes on the way up—whose entourages do not yet include savvy physiotherapists and doctors—don't overdose and do themselves damage.

EVALUATING THE AUTHORS' ARGUMENTS:

In this viewpoint Blue argues that legalizing steroids and other performance-enhancing drugs would do more to protect athletes than banning these substances. How do you think the author of the preceding viewpoint, Marissa Saltzman, might respond to this argument? Explain your answer using evidence from the texts.

Performance-Enhancing Drugs Violate the Spirit of the Game

"The illegal use of performance-enhancing substances poses a serious threat to the integrity of the game."

George J. Mitchell

In the following viewpoint George J. Mitchell argues that performance-enhancing drugs should be illegal so as to retain the spirit of sportsmanship in professional competitions. When athletes use steroids and other performance-enhancing drugs, they gain an unfair advantage over athletes who do not use drugs, Mitchell claims. In some instances, athletes lose their place on a team or have their records surpassed by drug users, which clouds the authenticity of the game. In order to level the playing field, all competitors should have equal opportunity to excel on the playing field. Mitchell further argues that drug use makes fans and spectators question the skills of all the athletes, which further erodes the spirit of the game. To preserve the integrity of all sports, steroids and performance-enhancing drugs should be illegal, Mitchell concludes.

Mitchell is a former Democratic senator from Maine. He is an author of four books as well as the author of an independent investigative report on the widespread use of steroids in Major League Baseball.

AS YOU READ, CONSIDER THE FOLLOWING QUESTIONS:
1. According to the author, former coach Dave McKay estimates what percentage of Major League Baseball players were using performance-enhancing drugs?
2. What does the author say is the biggest complaint among athletes about fellow athletes who use steroids?
3. How should the commissioner of baseball best handle steroid violations to protect the integrity of the game, according to the author?

For more than a decade there has been widespread illegal use of anabolic steroids and other performance-enhancing substances by players in Major League Baseball, in violation of federal law and baseball policy. Club officials routinely have discussed the possibility of such substance use when evaluating players. Those who have illegally used these substances range from players whose major league careers were brief to potential members of the Baseball Hall of Fame. They include both pitchers and position players, and their backgrounds are as diverse as those of all major league players. . . .

Who Is Using Steroids?

In 2002, former National League Most Valuable Player Ken Caminiti estimated that "at least half" of major league players were using anabolic steroids. Dave McKay, a longtime coach for the St. Louis Cardinals and the Oakland Athletics, estimated that at one time 30% of players were using them. Within the past week, the former Cincinnati Reds pitcher Jack Armstrong estimated that between 20% and 30% of players in his era, 1988 to 1994, were using large doses of steroids while an even higher percentage of players were using lower, maintenance doses of steroids. There have been other estimates, a few higher, many lower, all impossible to verify.

However, it is a fact that between 5 and 7 percent of the major league players who participated in anonymous survey testing in 2003 tested positive for performance-enhancing substances. Those figures almost certainly understated the actual level of use since players knew they would be tested at some time during the year, the use of human growth hormone was not detectable in the tests that were conducted, and, as many have observed, a negative test does not necessarily mean that a player has not been using performance-enhancing substances.

Mandatory random testing, formally started in 2004 after the survey testing results, appears to have reduced the use of detectable steroids, but players switched to human growth hormone precisely because it is not detectable. Players who use human growth hormone apparently believe that it assists their ability to recover from injuries and fatigue during the long baseball season; this also is a major reason why players used steroids. . . .

Performance-Enhancing Drugs Threaten the Integrity of the Game

The illegal use of performance-enhancing substances poses a serious threat to the integrity of the game. Widespread use by players of such substances unfairly disadvantages the honest athletes who refuse to use them and raises questions about the validity of baseball records. In addition, because they are breaking the law, users of these substances are vulnerable to drug dealers who might seek to exploit their knowledge through threats intended to affect the outcome of baseball games or otherwise.

The illegal use of these substances to improve athletic performance also carries with it potentially serious negative side effects on the human body. Steroid users place themselves at risk for psychiatric problems, cardiovascular and liver damage, drastic changes to their reproductive systems, musculoskeletal injury, and other problems. Users of human growth hormone risk cancer, harm to their reproductive health, cardiac and thyroid problems, and overgrowth of bone and connective tissue.

Young Athletes Are at Risk

Apart from the dangers posed to the major league player himself, however, his use of performance-enhancing substances encourages young athletes to use those substances. Young Americans are placing

Players Named in the Mitchell Report

The 2007 Mitchell Report is the result of former U.S. senator George J. Mitchell's twenty-month investigation into the use of anabolic steroids and human growth hormone (HGH) in Major League Baseball (MLB). The 409-page report named eighty-nine MLB players who have allegedly used steroids or other performance-enhancing drugs, including:

Manny Alexander	Troy Glaus	Andy Pettitte
Chad Allen	Juan Gonzalez	Adam Piatt
Rick Ankiel	Jason Grimsley	Todd Pratt
David Bell	Jose Guillen	Stephen Randolph
Mike Bell	Jerry Hairston Jr.	Adam Riggs
Marvin Benard	Matt Herges	Armando Rios
Gary Bennett Jr.	Phil Hiatt	Brian Roberts
Larry Bigbie	Glenallen Hill	John Rocker
Barry Bonds	Darren Holmes	F.P. Santangelo
Ricky Bones	Todd Hundley	Benito Santiago
Kevin Brown	Ryan Jorgensen	Scott Schoenweis
Paul Byrd	Wally Joyner	David Segui
Ken Caminiti	Mike Judd	Gary Sheffield
Jose Canseco	David Justice	Mike Stanton
Mark Carreon	Chuck Knobloch	Ricky Stone
Jason Christiansen	Tim Laker	Miguel Tejada
Howie Clark	Mike Lansing	Derrick Turnbow
Roger Clemens	Paul LoDuca	Ismael Valdez
Paxton Crawford	Exavier "Nook" Logan	Mo Vaughn
Jack Cust	Josias Manzanillo	Randy Velarde
Brendan Donnelly	Gary Matthews Jr.	Ron Villone
Chris Donnels	Mark McGwire	Fernando Vina
Lenny Dykstra	Cody McKay	Rondell White
Bobby Estalella	Kent Mercker	Jeff Williams
Matt Franco	Bart Miadich	Matt Williams
Ryan Franklin	Hal Morris	Todd Williams
Eric Gagne	Dan Naulty	Steve Woodard
Jason Giambi	Denny Neagle	Kevin Young
Jeremy Giambi	Rafael Palmeiro	Gregg Zaun
Jay Gibbons	Jim Parque	

themselves at risk of serious harm. Because adolescents are already subject to significant hormonal changes, the abuse of steroids and other performance-enhancing substances can have more serious effects on them than they have on adults.

Some estimates appear to show a recent decline in steroid use by high school students; they range from 3 to 6 percent. But even the lower figure means that hundreds of thousands of high school–aged young people are still illegally using steroids. It's important to devote attention to the Major League Baseball players who illegally used performance-enhancing substances. It's at least as important, perhaps even more so, to be concerned about the reality that hundreds of thousands of our children are using them. Every American, not just baseball fans, ought to be shocked into action by that disturbing truth. The recent decline is welcome, but we cannot be complacent.

Don Hooton, whose son committed suicide after abusing anabolic steroids, created the Taylor Hooton Foundation for Fighting Steroid Abuse. In 2005 congressional testimony, Mr. Hooton said:

> I believe the poor example being set by professional athletes is a major catalyst fueling the high usage of steroids amongst our kids. Our kids look up to these guys. They want to do the things the pros do to be successful.
>
> Our youngsters hear the message loud and clear, and it's wrong. "If you would want to achieve your goal, it's OK to use steroids to get you there, because the pros are doing it." It's a real challenge for parents to overpower the strong message that's being sent to our children by your behavior.

Steroid Use Is Not Fair to Clean Athletes

Finally, the illegal use in baseball of steroids and other performance-enhancing substances victimizes the majority of players who do not use those substances. A September 2000 study by the National Center on Addiction and Substance Abuse observed that:

> "Clean" athletes face three choices: (1) compete without performance-enhancing substances, knowing that they may lose to competitors with fewer scruples; (2) abandon their quest because they are unwill-

ing to use performance-enhancing substances to achieve a decisive competitive advantage; or (3) use performance-enhancing substances to level the playing field.

We heard from many former players who believed it was grossly unfair that some players were using performance-enhancing substances to gain an advantage. One former player told us that one of the "biggest complaints" among players was that a "guy is using steroids and he is taking my spot." . . .

What Should Be Done to Address Steroid Use?

Only the Commissioner [of baseball] is vested with authority to take disciplinary action. Any such determination is properly for the Commissioner to make, subject to the players' right to a hearing.

I urge the Commissioner to forego imposing discipline on players for past violations of baseball's rules on performance-enhancing substances, . . . except in those cases where he determines that the conduct is so serious that discipline is necessary to maintain the integrity of the game. I make this recommendation fully aware that there are valid arguments both for and against it; but I believe that those in favor are compelling. . . .

Most of the alleged violations in this report are distant in time. For current players, the allegations of possession or use are at least two, and as many as nine years old. This

> **FAST FACT**
>
> A March 2008 poll by the *New York Times* and CBS found that 34 percent of baseball fans believe at least half of all major league players use performance-enhancing drugs.

covers a period when Major League Baseball made numerous changes in its drug policies and program: it went from limited probable cause testing to mandatory random testing; since 2002, the penalties under the program have been increased several times; human growth hormone was not included as a prohibited substance under the joint drug program until 2005. Under basic principles of labor and employment law, an employer must apply the policies in place at the time of the conduct in question in determining what, if any, discipline is appropriate.

The Commissioner should give the players the chance to make a fresh start, except where the conduct is so serious that he must act to protect the integrity of the game. This would be a tangible and positive way for him to demonstrate to the players, to the clubs, to the fans, and to the general public his desire for the cooperative effort that baseball needs to deal effectively with this problem. It also would give him a clear and convincing basis for imposing meaningful discipline for future violations. . . .

The Spirit of the Game Should Be Restored

The minority of players who used such substances were wrong. They violated federal law and baseball policy, and they distorted the fairness of competition by trying to gain an unfair advantage over the

George J. Mitchell testifies before Congress about his findings in his investigation of the use of illegal steroids in Major League Baseball.

majority of players who followed the law and the rules. They—the players who follow the law and the rules—are faced with the painful choice of either being placed at a competitive disadvantage or becoming illegal users themselves. No one should have to make that choice.

EVALUATING THE AUTHOR'S ARGUMENTS:

George J. Mitchell argues that athletes who use steroids violate the spirit of the game, erode fair competition, and insult fellow athletes. As a result, he believes that all performance-enhancing drugs must be made illegal to return integrity to sportsmanship and competition. Clarify what he means by this. Do you think he is right? Explain your answer thoroughly.

Viewpoint
4

Performance-Enhancing Drugs Make for More Entertaining Games

Eugene Robinson

"We, the paying customers, don't want normal-size athletes with normal abilities. We want to see supermen and superwomen performing super feats."

In the following viewpoint Eugene Robinson argues that athletes who use performance-enhancing drugs make sports more exciting. Most fans watch sports, Robinson claims, to see people unlike themselves perform extraordinary physical feats. The superhuman quality of professional athletes is precisely what Americans admire about them. As more records are broken, athletes face pressure to become faster and stronger than their predecessors, Robinson explains. They therefore turn to performance-enhancing drugs for an extra boost that will push them to the next skill level. Robinson concludes by saying that athletes who choose to take performance-enhancing drugs do so to provide the ultimate entertainment for their fans.

Robinson is an associate editor and twice-weekly columnist for the *Washington Post*.

AS YOU READ, CONSIDER THE FOLLOWING QUESTIONS:
1. What does the author mean when he says that Barry Bonds' steroid use makes him "simply a man of his age?"
2. According to the author, what percentage of professional baseball players use or have used performance-enhancing substances?
3. Why are fans and spectators willing to pay athletes high salaries, according to the author?

L et's take a brief respite from politics to consider the elasticity of human potential:

On April 2, 2002, the Los Angeles Dodgers [baseball team] played a home game against the San Francisco Giants. In the top of the second inning, with two men on base, Dodgers ace Kevin Brown had to face slugger Barry Bonds. Brown blew his first pitch past the game's best hitter for a called strike. Bonds slammed Brown's second pitch over the left-center-field fence—his first home run of the year, and number 568 in his career.

Leveling the Playing Field

It is now assumed, of course, that Bonds may have been juiced on steroids at the time; the previous year he had set the all-time single-season record of 73 home runs, and his musculature was almost freakishly swollen. But even the baseball fundamentalists who want to excise all of Bonds' suspect home runs from the record books should make an exception for number 568, right? Because we now have an allegation that Brown was juiced, too—on human growth hormone and maybe steroids. If both pitcher and batter are artificially enhanced, doesn't that level the playing field?

Steroid Use in Baseball Is Widespread

Brown is one of more than 90 major league players mentioned in former Sen. George Mitchell's voluminous report on the problem of steroids and other performance-enhancing drugs in the sport once considered our national pastime.

It is now assumed that when Barry Bonds broke Major League Baseball's single-season home run record in 2001 he was "juiced" on steroids.

According to the report, Kirk Radomski—a former New York Mets batboy, equipment manager and hanger-on who became a kind of Dr. Feelgood to the stars—says he routinely shipped quantities of growth hormone to Brown via overnight mail. He claims that Brown, who declined to be interviewed by Mitchell, shipped back wads of cash as payment.

Last summer, as Bonds closed in on the all-time home run record and baseball purists were all but calling for him to be hauled away and waterboarded, I wrote that in terms of steroid use, Bonds was "simply a man of his age." That was an understatement, it turns out.

Steroid abusers in baseball "range from players whose major league careers were brief to potential members of the Baseball Hall of Fame," Mitchell reported. He said he could not establish how many players used performance-enhancing substances, but he quotes estimates by former players that range from 20 percent to "at least half." And among the players specifically named are 31 pitchers—including the best pitcher of our time, Roger Clemens, who denies the allegation.

Athletes Who Use Performance-Enhancing Drugs Are Exciting to Watch

Let me be clear: People shouldn't abuse steroids or growth hormones in an effort to improve their athletic performance. These substances are bad for you. They are especially dangerous for kids who seek to emulate their athletic heroes by bulking up to Schwarzeneggerian proportions.

But what about eye surgery? To switch sports for a moment, golfer Tiger Woods had laser surgery that not only remedied his nearsightedness but actually gave him better than 20-20 vision.

Have any major leaguers with normal vision gone under the laser in an attempt to gain an edge? Wouldn't submitting healthy eyes to a performance-enhancing operation be just as problematic?

To switch sports again, as the college and professional football seasons wrap up with bowl games and playoffs, note the size of the linemen. Anything under 300 pounds is considered "small." Of course, it's not really healthy to carry around that much weight—and players pay the price when

> **FAST FACT**
>
> According to a poll conducted by MSN-Zogby, 38 percent of American adults report that their enjoyment of watching sports is not affected by the possibility that the athletes are using performance-enhancing drugs.

their football careers are over. Yet you can now see 300-pound linemen playing for elite high-school programs.

My point is that we, the paying customers, don't want normal-size athletes with normal abilities. We want to see supermen and superwomen performing super feats, and we're willing to pay these gladiators a fortune. Why should they disappoint us? Why should we expect them to?

EVALUATING THE AUTHOR'S ARGUMENTS:

In this viewpoint the author compares laser eye surgery to taking steroids as a way for athletes to gain an edge over their competitors. Do you agree with this comparison? Why or why not?

Viewpoint

5

Athletes Cheat When They Use Steroids

"Bonds has denied ever knowingly taking steroids. He has testified that he believed a clear substance and cream given [to] him by his trainer were flaxseed oil and an arthritis balm."

Peter Grier and Christa Case

In the following viewpoint, Peter Grier and Christa Case argue that athletes cheat when they use performance-enhancing drugs. This is especially true when athletes Marion Jones and Barry Bonds had set all-time records—possibly as a result of steroid use. Athletes are finding it increasingly difficult to remain unnoticed as new coalitions of law-enforcement and watchdog agencies are working to clean up sports and force athletes to return medals and revoke honors.

Peter Grier and Christa Case are staff writers of the *Christian Science Monitor*.

AS YOU READ, CONSIDER THE FOLLOWING QUESTIONS:

1. According to the authors, how did Marion Jones cheat when she won Olympic medals in the Sidney Games?
2. What do the authors mean when they say "the fact that she was caught by law enforcement should be a warning"?
3. Why do the authors convey that Marion Jones' tearful admission leaves many questions unanswered?

Peter Grier and Christa Case, "Marion Jones Caught by a Wider Antidoping Net," *Christian Science Monitor*, October 10, 2007, p. 1. Copyright © 2007 The Christian Science Publishing Society. All rights reserved. Reproduced by permission from *Christian Science Monitor* (www.csmonitor.com).

D rug-cheat athletes beware: You can lose your career, your trophies, and your reputation even if you don't fail an actual drug test.

That may be one vital lesson from the sad case of Olympian Marion Jones, say antidoping experts and officials.

Coming Clean

New coalitions of law-enforcement and watchdog agencies are working to clean up sports, they say. They can draw on invoices, shipment records, and other evidence not related to testing regimens. Thus Jones's fall from grace may mark a new era in the fight to keep athletics free of performance-enhancing substances.

"[Jones] has been competing for many years and had delivered many samples, and none of them tested positive," says David Howman, director general of the World Anti-Doping Agency [WADA] in Montreal. "Now we have that extra armory of enforcement agencies, and that's probably the only reason that [she] confessed."

On Oct. 8, Jones handed back five Olympic medals won seven years ago in the Sydney Games. In addition, she agreed to forfeit all winning results dating back to Sept. 1, 2000.

FAST FACT

A poll published on PollingPoint.com found that 79 percent of respondents believe steroid use is a major problem in sports.

The US Olympic Committee will return the medals to the International Olympic Committee, which will decide what to do with them. After long denying she had ever used performance enhancers, Jones admitted Friday that she'd taken the designer steroid "the clear" from September 2000 to July 2001. "The clear" has been linked to BALCO, the lab at the center of the steroids scandal in professional sports.

Her admission came as part of a guilty plea to lying to federal investigators about using steroids. She will be sentenced early in 2008 and could get up to six months in prison.

Jones is now one of the highest-profile figures to be snared by the government's long-running BALCO investigation. Home-run king

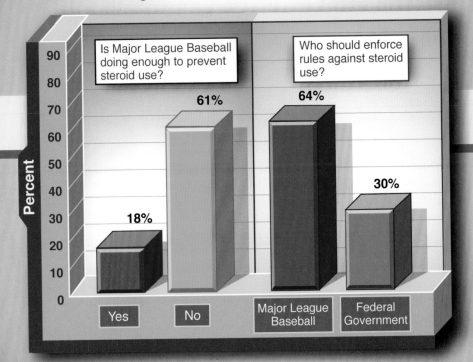

Steroids in Baseball

A March 2005 poll found that most Americans think Major League Baseball is not doing enough to curb steroid use in the sport.

Is Major League Baseball doing enough to prevent steroid use?

Who should enforce rules against steroid use?

61%

64%

18%

30%

Yes

No

Major League Baseball

Federal Government

Percent

90
80
70
60
50
40
30
20
10
0

Taken from: ABC News/ESPN poll, March 2005.

Barry Bonds has been linked to the case, and a grand jury is still investigating whether he lied to federal investigators.

Bonds has denied ever knowingly taking steroids. He has testified that he believed a clear substance and cream given him by his trainer were flaxseed oil and an arthritis balm.

Jones has been dogged by rumors of steroid use for years. An ex-husband and an ex-boyfriend, both athletes, have been caught doping by sports authorities.

Yet Jones herself has not completely failed any drug test. In 2006, one test showed traces of the hormone-boosting substance EPO [Erythropoietin], but a backup "B" sample came up clear, allowing her at the time to claim vindication.

When Barry Bonds hit his 756th home run to break the career home run record, many felt that the record was tainted because of Bond's alleged use of performance-enhancing drugs.

Consequences of Steroid Use

Her tearful admission of wrongdoing and apology to family and friends leave many questions unanswered. But her loss of medals and possible loss of earnings is a heavy blow, note antidoping officials. "[Her] punishment is in line with the rules but also with the offenses," says Travis Tygart, senior managing director and general counsel of the US Anti-Doping Agency.

And the fact that she was caught by law enforcement should be a warning, add sport officials. For the last two years, the World Anti-Doping Agency has been working with police and other government agencies to crack down on doping, notes the organization's director general.

Since WADA is a nongovernmental organization, countries cannot use its antidoping code to prosecute individuals involved in doping, explains Mr. Howman. But 67 countries have now ratified a UNESCO [United Nations Educational, Scientific and Cultural Organization] convention drawn up in 2005 that serves as a tool for governments seeking to curb doping in sport. Also, WADA is exploring cooperation with Interpol, which would allow police in any country with laws against trafficking in steroids to share information with each other.

Similar cooperation has led to the sanction of athletes based on evidence gathered outside urine and blood tests.

Global Steroid Use Among Athletes

In Australia, for example, five athletes have been prosecuted for possession of human growth hormone (HGH) after being snared by a customs agency. With evidence collected by Italian police during a raid at the 2006 Turin Olympic Games, four Austrian cross-country skiers and two biathletes were issued lifetime bans early this year.

The cross-country skiers have appealed their cases. That incident marked the first time the International Olympic Committee had disqualified athletes for doping violations with positive tests.

Now, WADA is involved in Spain's Operation Puerto case, which uncovered an apparent blood-doping operation that was linked with numerous cyclists, including German star Jan Ullrich.

No athletes have been prosecuted under Operation Puerto, and the cases are still under appeal.

The challenge in such cases, notes Howman, is that in many cases, "prosecutors are not really that interested in the end users [athletes]. They're more interested in traffickers and doctors."

EVALUATING THE AUTHORS' ARGUMENTS:

In this viewpoint the authors argue that athletes who use steroids and other performance-enhancing drugs cheat, especially when their drug use lands them in the record books. As of late, these athletes are being caught and punished at a higher rate and losing it all. What pieces of evidence do the authors provide to support their claim? Did they convince you of their argument? Why or why not?

Steroid Use Is Not Cheating

Jacob Sullum

In the following viewpoint Jacob Sullum argues that athletes do not cheat when they use steroids to improve their athletic performance. While opponents argue that athletes gain an unfair advantage when they use performance-enhancing drugs, Sullum says that steroids are merely an evolution in sport. In fact, Sullum compares steroid use to fitness knowledge, nutritional expertise, and state-of-the-art exercise equipment— these, like performance-enhancing drugs, are just the latest tools to help an athlete achieve his or her maximum potential. Athletes should not be penalized for choosing to use performance-enhancing drugs and should definitely not be banned from the sport or have their records deleted, Sullum claims. He concludes that steroids should be legal and available to all athletes so that those who choose to use them would not be unfairly persecuted.

Sullum is a senior editor of *Reason*, a monthly libertarian magazine. He is also the author of two books: *Saying Yes: In Defense of Drug Use* and *For Your Own Good: The Anti-Smoking Crusade and the Tyranny of Public Health.*

"Using drugs to boost performance is cheating only if it violates a rule."

In one of the more puzzling parts of his State of the Union speech, President [George W.] Bush offered his opinion about how professional sports should be run. He did not criticize the instant replay rule, condemn the use of designated hitters, or tell returning head coach Joe Gibbs how to restore the Redskins [football team] to their former glory. Instead, he asserted that athletes should not be permitted to use "performance-enhancing drugs like steroids."

Bush stated this principle as if it were obviously true, as if no reasonable person could disagree that "team owners, union representatives, coaches, and players" need to "get rid of steroids now." Yet the more you think about it, the less sense there is to a rule that prohibits athletes from using drugs to enhance their performance.

The Dangers of Steroids Are Exaggerated

One reason the president offered is that such drugs are "dangerous." Compared to what? Football players routinely get knocked around by 300-pound behemoths. They and other professional athletes frequently suffer injuries—pulled hamstrings, concussions, torn ligaments, busted knees, separated shoulders—that may force them out of the game for months or leave them with lifelong disabilities. If avoiding danger were their main concern, they would not be playing to begin with.

In any case, as sports writer Dayn Perry shows in the January 2003 issue of *Reason*, the hazards of anabolic steroids have been greatly exaggerated. After looking at the scientific literature and interviewing experts, Perry concludes that steroids can be used with reasonable safety by adults under medical supervision.

The irony is that legal restrictions and league bans on steroids discourage athletes who use them from seeking medical guidance, so

President Bush has stated that athletes should not use performance-enhancing drugs in baseball but left it up to Major League Baseball officials to address the problems.

they're more at risk than they would be if steroid use were permitted. As with recreational drugs, prohibition makes steroids *more* dangerous, not less.

Like Steroids, Talent Is a Shortcut to Accomplishment

Safety was not the only issue the president raised. He also said using performance-enhancing drugs "sends the wrong message: that there are shortcuts to accomplishment, and that performance is more important than character."

A man who owes so much to inherited wealth and his family's political connections probably should not broach the topic of "shortcuts to accomplishment." Not all shortcuts come in pills or capsules.

An athlete who uses the latest exercise equipment, fitness knowledge, and nutritional expertise to get into shape is using shortcuts that were unavailable to his predecessors 30 or 40 years ago. More fundamentally, all professional athletes benefit from the shortcut known as talent: Because of their genetic endowments, they are stronger, faster, or more agile than most people.

Athletes, like everyone else, are rightly judged by what they do with the advantages they had at birth. But if their innate abilities do not negate their accomplishments, why would their use of artificial enhancements that are available to everyone?

All Athletes Should Be Allowed to Use Steroids

Craig Masback, chief executive of USA Track and Field, praised Bush's anti-steroid comments, saying "cheating by our star athletes sends the wrong message." Yet using drugs to boost performance is cheating only if it violates a rule, such as the ban on steroids maintained by the Olympics and the NFL.

If all athletes were allowed to use chemical aids, those who chose to do so would not have an unfair advantage any more than an actress with breast implants does. And just as it is possible to enjoy an actress's performance despite her artificial enhancements, it should be possible to enjoy a football or baseball game despite the use of steroids or stimulants—and obviously it is, since fan interest in these sports has not exactly evaporated in recent years, despite periodic doping scandals.

> **FAST FACT**
>
> A 2007 study of two thousand American men who used anabolic steroids, published by the *Journal of the International Society of Sports Nutrition*, found that only 6 percent used the drugs for athletic or bodybuilding purposes.

"No result in any elite sport can be trusted with reasonable certainty to have been achieved without performance-enhancing drugs," *New York Times* sports writer Jere Longman declared last fall. At the same time, he conceded, "whether fans believe this or care is another matter."

Donald Catlin, director of the Olympic drug testing lab at UCLA, told Longman, "In a way, if all the top athletes were on drugs, they would be on an equal footing again." While Catlin views that prospect with distaste, it's not clear why.

It's Difficult to Justify Banning Steroids

Two decades ago, in their book *Drug Control in a Free Society*, James B. Bakalar and Lester Grinspoon noted that "it seems almost self-evident to most people today that using drugs in athletic competition is wrong," but "it is curiously difficult and complicated to justify that position." A presidential endorsement does not make the task any easier.

> ## EVALUATING THE AUTHORS' ARGUMENTS:
>
> In this viewpoint Sullum argues that athletes should be allowed to use steroids to improve their athletic performance. The authors of the preceding viewpoint, Grier and Case, say that athletes cheat when they use performance-enhancing drugs. With which perspective do you agree? Why?

Chapter 2

What Consequences Should Exist for Athletes Who Use Drugs?

Urine samples await to be tested at UCLA's Olympic Analytical Laboratory in Los Angeles, CA. The lab tests over 40,000 samples a year supplied by athletes.

Viewpoint

1

Harsher Penalties Are Needed for Athletes Who Use Drugs

Mark Sappenfield

"Major League Baseball has been transformed from American pro sports' most profligate flouter of performance-enhancing drug policy to their pioneer."

In the following viewpoint, Mark Sappenfield argues that athletes who use performance-enhancing drugs are facing more severe penalties for their actions. In his opinion, movements like the Olympic Games monitoring system has discovered drug testing is an ever-evolving underworld of new substances and masking techniques. Sappenfield concludes that professional sports organizations like Major League Baseball and the U.S. Congress are in agreement on tough penalties for athletic drug use.

Mark Sappenfield is a staff writer for the *Christian Science Monitor*.

Mark Sappenfield, "Baseball Takes Lead on Drug Testing, Now the Hard Part: Catching Cheats Will Require Tough—and Expensive—Monitoring," *Christian Science Monitor*, November 17, 2005. Copyright © 2005 The Christian Science Publishing Society. All rights reserved. Reproduced by permission from *Christian Science Monitor* (www.csmonitor.com).

AS YOU READ, CONSIDER THE FOLLOWING QUESTIONS:
1. According to the author, who has the toughest penalties for pro athletes being caught using performance-enhancing drugs?
2. What does the author mean when he says "The major leagues have now entered this arena in earnest"?
3. What proof does the author give for the statement "After two years of baseball being on the offensive against steroids, there are signs of improvement, at least for the moment."

E ven to its critics, Major League Baseball's new antidoping policy is no small thing. To be sure, there were factors outside baseball's good intentions to move the process forward—not least an international scandal that tainted Olympic sprinters and baseball sluggers alike, and Congress's not-so-subtle attentions.

A New Era

Yet the fact remains that in the space of a single season, Major League Baseball has been transformed from American pro sports' most profligate flouter of performance-enhancing drug policy to their pioneer. In the process, the league has overturned the deep reservations of what has been called the country's most powerful union—the players'

association—and weathered repeated allegations that some of the most accomplished players of its recent past were drug cheats.

Now, however, comes the hard part. As the Olympic movement has discovered, drug testing is an ever-evolving underworld of new substances and masking techniques. Even under the best circumstances, the testers are always a step behind.

The major leagues have now entered this arena in earnest, and the success of this week's pact—if it is ratified as expected—will depend on baseball's desire to adapt and reform after the browbeating ends.

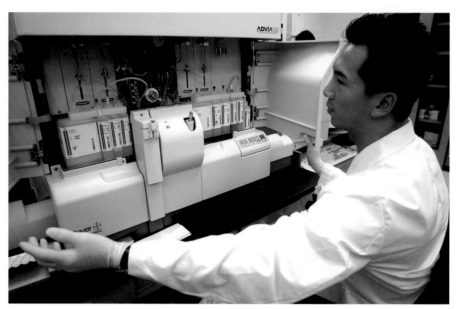

A technician at the UCLA Olympic Analytical Laboratory tests an athlete's blood sample for banned substances.

"This is a work in progress," says Gary Wadler, who works with the World Anti-Doping Agency and has testified before Congress on the issue of performance-enhancing drugs. "It has to be monitored—both its details and the implementation of the details."

Broad Strokes

Those details are not yet clear. The plan presented by baseball officials Tuesday lays out the leagues' new guidelines in broad strokes. Yet some of these broad strokes, in and of themselves, are groundbreaking.

The penalties, though still below the Olympic standard, are now the toughest in American team sports: 50 days' suspension for a first positive test, 100 days for a second, and a lifetime ban for a third—with the possibility of backdoor reinstatement through the commissioner after two years. Perhaps more significant, baseball also took on amphetamine—stimulants known to be used widely in baseball for years.

"You have to at least condemn [these drugs]," says Ken Rosenthal of FOXSports.com. "Now, at least they're on the right side."

At this point, it seems that Congress is on their side, too. At a Monitor breakfast Wednesday, Rep. Tom Davis (R) of Virginia, who

Testing Policies and Penalties for Performance-Enhancing Drugs

As of 2007, five major sports networks enforced penalties for using performance-enhancing drugs such as steroids and human growth hormone (HGH).

Major League Baseball

At least two annual urine tests administered during and between seasons for anabolic steroids and amphetamines. Positive steroid tests result in a 50-game suspension for a first offense, a 100-game suspension for a second offense, and a lifetime ban for a third offense.

NFL

Urine tests administered randomly during the season or off-season for anabolic steroids and amphetamines. Players must be tested at least once a year. Four-game suspension for a first positive steroid test, six-game suspension for a second positive test, and a full season for a third positive test.

NBA

Urine tests administered four times randomly during the season for steroids and amphetamines. Ten-game suspension for a first positive test, 25-game suspension for a second positive, one year for a third, and a lifetime ban for a fourth. Congress has criticized the policy for not addressing human growth hormone or designer steroids.

NHL

Players subject to a maximum two tests during the season for performance-enhancing drugs. Twenty-game suspension for a first offense, 60-game suspension for a second offense, and lifetime ban for a third offense. Congress has criticized the policy for not requiring annual tests and not including designer steroids.

Olympics

All Olympic sports adhere to the World Anti-Doping Agency list of banned substances. Athletes can be tested at random while not in competition and at international events. Blood and urine tests are used. First positive results in a minimum two-year suspension and the second in a lifetime ban.

Taken from: Childs Walker, "Testing Policies and Penalties for Performance-Enhancing Drugs," *Baltimore Sun*, December 14, 2007.

chaired Congress's steroid hearings in the spring, said baseball's new policies were a victory. "This is a huge sea change," he said.

But he also suggested that he and other lawmakers would keep a close eye on baseball's progress. The list of which drugs will be banned is not complete; nor is it clear what the relationship will be between baseball and the new independent investigator responsible for carrying out drug tests.

Signs of Improvement

After two years of baseball being on the offensive against steroids, there are signs of improvement, at least for the moment. From 1995 to 2002—the height of the so-called Steroid Era—at least one player hit 50 home runs each year, including four players in 1998, the year Mark McGwire hit 70 to break the single-season home-run record. The past two years, no one has hit more than 48.

But to stay on the offensive without Congress's constant threats could be difficult. In many ways, the fans are at best ambivalent about the issue; the steroid scandals of recent years have not affected sales at the gate. That means the pressure to continue to evolve baseball's drug policy—which could mean millions of dollars in research and renewed battles with the players' union—will fall on baseball itself.

Says Dr. Wadler: "The accountability must be there."

EVALUATING THE AUTHOR'S ARGUMENTS:

In this viewpoint the author argues that athletes who use steroids and other performance-enhancing drugs are being caught and punished more severely by their sport and government monitors. Do you think this is a fair process for athletes who test positive for performance-enhancing drugs? If yes, explain your reasoning. If no, suggest other ways athletes might be dealt with if they violate antidrug rules.

Athletes Who Use Drugs Should Not Be Penalized

Bengt Kayser, Alexandre Mauron, and Andy Miah

"We believe that rather than drive doping underground, use of drugs should be permitted under medical supervision."

In the following viewpoint Bengt Kayser, Alexandre Mauron, and Andy Miah argue that athletes should not be penalized for using performance-enhancing drugs. While they acknowledge that current antidrug policies are designed to promote fair play in sports, in actuality these policies are often ethically misguided, costly, and dangerous. While supporters of antidoping regulation claim that performance-enhancing drugs give athletes an unfair advantage, the authors argue it is impossible to ever have a truly balanced playing field: differing biological and environmental conditions also provide advantages to athletes. It is unwise to ignore these advantages in some athletes while punishing others for finding alternative ways to improve their game. As such, the authors conclude that antidrug policies in sports are inadequate, unfair, and ineffective.

Kayser is professor of exercise physiology and Mauron is professor of bioethics at the Faculty of Medicine of the University of Geneva in Switzerland. Miah is a lecturer of bioethics and cyberculture at the University of Paisley in the United Kingdom. He is also the author of the book *Genetically Modified Athletes, Biomedical Ethics, Gene Doping and Sport.*

AS YOU READ, CONSIDER THE FOLLOWING QUESTIONS:
1. In the authors' opinion, why is drug use in sports not any more dangerous than the sports themselves?
2. Why do the authors believe that legalizing performance-enhancing drugs will reduce health problems associated with those drugs?
3. What two reasons do the authors give for prohibiting performance-enhancing drugs being more problematic than beneficial?

T he rules of sport define level playing field on which athletes compete. Antidoping policies exist, in theory, to encourage fair play. However, we believe they are unfounded, dangerous, and excessively costly.

Antidrug Regulations in Sports Are Misguided

The need for rules in sports cannot be dismissed. But the anchoring of today's antidoping regulations in the notion of fair play is misguided, since other factors that affect performance—eg, biological and environmental factors—are unchecked. Getting help from one's genes—by being blessed with a performance-enhancing genetic predisposition—is acceptable. Use of drugs is not. Yet both types of advantage are undeserved. Prevailing sports ethics is unconcerned with this contradiction.

"Sport Is Dangerous Even if No Drugs Are Taken"

Another ethical foundation for antidoping concerns the athlete's health. Antidoping control is judged necessary to prevent damage from doping. However, sport is dangerous even if no drugs are taken—playing soccer comes with high risks for knee and ankle problems, for instance, and boxing can lead to brain damage. To comprehensively assess any increase in risk afforded by the use of drugs or technology, every performance-enhancing method needs to be studied. Such work cannot be done while use of drugs performance-enhancing drugs is illegal. We believe that rather than drive doping underground, use of drugs should be permitted under medical supervision.

Medical Supervision of Drug Use in Sports Would Be Safer

Legalisation of the use of drugs in sport might even have some advantages. The boundary between the therapeutic and ergogenic—ie, performance enhancing—use of drugs is blurred at present and poses difficult questions for the controlling bodies of antidoping practice and for sports doctors. The antidoping rules often lead to complicated and costly administrative and medical follow-up to ascertain whether drugs taken by athletes are legitimate therapeutic agents or illicit.

Progress Is Being Made Against Steroid Use in Sports

In July 2006, the NCAA Committee on Competitive Safeguards and Medical Aspects of Sports released data from a five-year report showing that positive steroid tests in the NCAA collegiate ranks have made notable decreases since 2000.

2000–2001	93 positive tests
2001–2002	71 positive tests
2002–2003	80 positive tests
2003–2004	46 positive tests
2004–2005	49 positive tests

Taken from: NCAA Committee on Competitive Safeguards and Medical Aspects of Sports, July 2006.

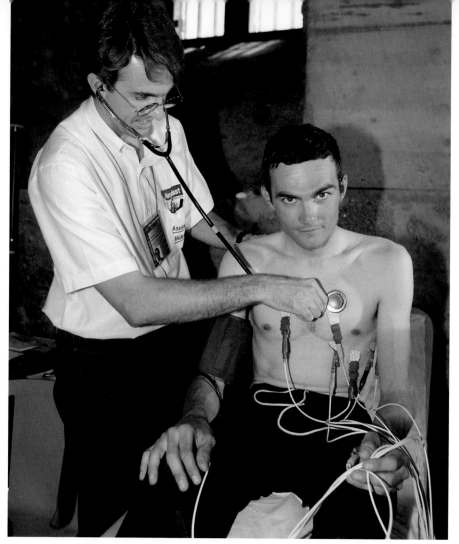

A sports doctor has to preserve the patient's best interest with respect to their health while maintaining the athlete's performance at a high level.

If doping was allowed, would there be an increase in the rate of death and chronic illness among athletes? Would athletes have a shorter lifespan than the general population? Would there be more examples like the widespread use of performance-enhancing drugs in the former East-German republic? We do not think so. Only a small proportion of the population engages in elite sports. Furthermore, legalization of doping, we believe, would encourage more sensible, informed use of drugs in amateur sport, leading to an overall decline in the rate of health problems associated with doping. Finally, by allowing medically supervised doping, the drugs used could be assessed for a clearer view of what is dangerous and what is not.

Athletes Should Not Be Penalized for Using Performance-Enhancing Drugs

The role of the doctor is to preserve their patients' best interests with respect to present and future health. A sports doctor has to fulfil this role while maintaining the athlete's performance at as high a level as possible. As such, as long as the first condition is met, any intervention proven safe, pharmacological or otherwise, should be justified, irrespective of whether or not it is ergogenic. A doctor who tries to enhance the performance of their athlete should not be punished for the use of pharmacological aids, but should be held accountable for any ill effects. Rather than speculate on antidoping test procedures, resources should be invested into protecting the integrity of doctors who make such judgments.

Acknowledging the importance of rules in sports, which might include the prohibition of doping, is, in itself, not problematic. However, a problem arises when the application of these rules is beset with diminishing returns: escalating costs and questionable effectiveness. The ethical foundation of prohibiting the use of ergogenic substances in sports is weak. As the cost of antidoping control rises year on year, ethical objections are raised that are in our view, weightier than the ethical arguments advanced for antidoping. In the competition between increasingly sophisticated doping—eg, gene transfer—and antidoping technology, there will never be a clear winner. Consequently, such a futile but expensive strategy is difficult to defend.

EVALUATING THE AUTHORS' ARGUMENTS:

In this viewpoint authors Kayser, Mauron, and Miah argue that athletes should not be penalized for using performance-enhancing drugs. How do you think the author of the preceding argument, Mark Sappenfield, might respond to this argument? Explain your answer using evidence from the texts.

Viewpoint
3

Athletes Who Use Drugs Should Have Their Records Deleted

"It's time for baseball to delete the asterisk from Barry Bonds' records and do what USA Track and Field and the Olympics would do —remove his records altogether."

Robert Weiner

In the following viewpoint Robert Weiner argues that athletes who use performance-enhancing drugs should have their names removed from athletic records. In recent years many athletes have turned to drugs to improve their performance. As a result, many have beaten all-time sports records. However, Weiner argues, it is unfair to athletes who earned their records with natural talent to be surpassed by athletes who artificially made themselves stronger and faster. A stringent zero tolerance drug policy should exist for all sports, Weiner claims, and any athlete who tests positive for performance-enhancing drugs should have their record erased from the books. Weiner believes that this is the most effective way to promote and restore fairness in all athletics.

Weiner was spokesman for the White House National Drug Policy Office from

1995 to 2001 and directed White House drug policy media at the Sydney Olympics and World Anti-Doping Agency media at the Salt Lake City Olympics.

AS YOU READ, CONSIDER THE FOLLOWING QUESTIONS:
1. How many student athletes have taken steroids, according to the U.S. Centers for Disease Control?
2. What sport has a "zero tolerance" drug policy that the author feels all sports participants should be subject to follow?
3. According to the author, enforcing antidrug policies sends what message to young athletes?

If Barry Bonds were subject to the rules of track and field—America's premier Olympic sport, holding its national convention in Honolulu this week [November 2007]—his home-run records would be "going, going, gone," as famed announcer Mel Allen used to say as the ball sailed out of the park. There would be no asterisk—Bonds' record would be annulled. Henry Aaron would be given back his hard-fought 1974 record of 755—and that's just what baseball should do.

Many Sports Downplay Performance-Enhancing Drug Use

For participants in the USA Track and Field Convention—national, state and local association chairpersons, meet organizers, officials, coaches and athletes young and old—no decision or action will have more impact than maintaining a strong anti-drug policy for our nation's youth, especially approaching the Beijing Olympics.

Bonds has increased his hat, shoe and chest sizes by 25 percent during the last 10 years, from ages 33–43, not exactly a young boy's growing period. *Time* magazine reported Bonds' swelling up as "a telltale sign of human growth hormone," or HGH. For him to say he didn't "knowingly" take drugs defies what everyone knows that human growth hormone and steroids do.

After a positive test result, Bonds publicly admitted taking amphetamines, but predictably claimed he didn't know what it was when he got it from a teammate. Still baseball did not penalize him.

Bonds was indicted November 2007 for perjury and obstruction of justice for testifying before a federal grand jury in 2003 that he never used performance-enhancing drugs.

Baseball players and coaches downplay amphetamine pills as unimportant "greenies" despite the aggressive, criminal and suicidal tendencies they engender when not medically monitored.

Performance-Enhancing Drugs Are Dangerous

The U.S. Centers for Disease Control report that one million student athletes say they have taken steroids. After former St. Louis Cardinals' home run hitter Mark McGwire tested positive for Androstenedione or "Andro" (now labeled a steroid), sales of the drug quadrupled, confirming a Kaiser Foundation finding that three-quarters of kids say they look up to and want to emulate professional athletes.

FAST FACT

According to an article in *USA Today*, three American Olympic athletes have lost their medals due to positive drug tests: Marion Jones, Jerome Young, and Rick DeMont.

Before children start taking steroids and HGH, they need to be aware of the real harm and dangerous side effects, including liver and heart disease, cancer, shrunken body parts, hair in the wrong places, suicide (many sad parents recently testified before Congress) and, as the family of wrestler Chris Benoit can attest, paranoid, schizophrenic, murderous rages. Thousands of East German swimmers are now suing the current government for illnesses from forced steroid drugging.

All Sports Should Have a Zero Tolerance Policy for Performance-Enhancing Drugs

USA Track and Field, led by CEO Craig Masback and National Chairman Bill Roe, has a "zero tolerance" policy for performance-enhancing drugs and the most rigorous testing program in sport. The punishment of at least a two-year ban from competition and the annulment of results hurts, and is imposed even if the illegal users are

Barry Bonds enters court to answer charges of perjury and obstruction of justice for falsely testifying before a federal grand jury.

stars such as Olympic quintuple-medalist Marion Jones or 100-meter world record holder Tim Montgomery. Only in track and field is the entire entourage—coaches, doctors, trainers, assistants—equally subject to being banned.

Major League Baseball, on the other hand, has a "zero action" policy: do nothing unless boxed into a corner. It does not record tests

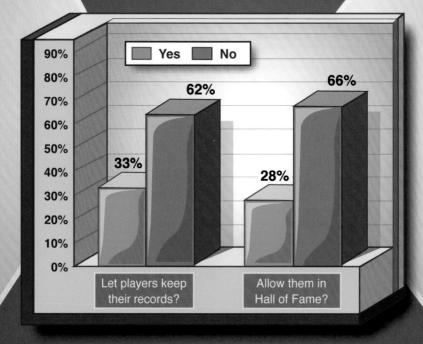

American Opinions About Penalties for Steroid Use

A 2005 poll found that the majority of Americans believe athletes caught using performance-enhancing drugs should lose their records and be banned from the Hall of Fame.

Yes ▢ No

90%
80%
70%
60%
50%
40%
30%
20%
10%
0%

62%

66%

33%

28%

Let players keep their records?

Allow them in Hall of Fame?

Taken from: ABC News/ESPN Poll, 2005.

for amphetamines, it secretly announces to teams at least a day before when "unannounced" steroid testers are coming (allowing players to disappear or use drug-masking agents) and does not seek information about HGH. The MLB investigation into steroid use now being conducted by former Sen. George Mitchell of Maine will provide generalities but no real action—and no unknown names will be named, according to the ground rules. Professional football, hockey, basketball and soccer are not much better—the objective of all pro sports seems to be to hide rather than block and punish drug abuse.

Drug Use in Sports Is Cheating

In helping to create the new World and U.S. Anti-Doping Agencies, former drug czar and retired four-star general Barry McCaffrey urged "open, accountable" drug policies that the world could see, hear and know. McCaffrey, outgoing WADA Chairman Dick Pound, and former USADA Chairman and Olympic marathon champion Frank Shorter—the triumvirate who launched the struggle against sports drug abuse—forcefully asserted that the era of hiding our embarrassments must be over. Youths must see and hear the point of drug-free athletics.

It's been a bad year [2007] for high-profile sports drug busts—not just Jones and Bonds, but Tour de France leader Michael Rasmussen and ex-Wimbledon tennis champion Martina Hingis among many others—but it's been a good year for letting the world know that drugs in sport are unacceptable. Every bust is a message to kids: Do not cheat.

Deleting Sports Records Encourages Youths to Avoid Performance-Enhancing Drugs

It's appalling for Bonds to assert, "This record is in no way tainted." It's time for baseball to delete the asterisk from Barry Bonds' records and do what USA Track and Field and the Olympics would do— remove his records altogether. It's time for other sports, sponsors and the media to step up and help. Because of the powerful symbolism of the baseball home-run record—like no other—it's the best way baseball can restore its integrity and join track and field in sending a loud and clear message for drug-free sport to youths and the nation.

EVALUATING THE AUTHOR'S ARGUMENTS:

The author of this viewpoint, Robert Weiner, was a spokesman for the White House National Drug Policy Office for six years and directed drug policy for both the Sydney Olympics and the Salt Lake City Olympics. Does knowing the background of this author influence your opinion of his argument? In what way?

Viewpoint

4

Imposing Penalties on Athletes Who Use Drugs Is Hypocritical

Colman McCarthy

"What's the difference between athletes juicing themselves with steroids and drunken fans in the stands doping themselves with the alcohol drug?"

In the following viewpoint Colman McCarthy argues that punishing athletes who use performance-enhancing drugs is hypocritical. McCarthy suggests that all kinds of drugs—from alcohol to coffee to Viagra—are used to enhance people's experiences every day. These drugs are similar to performance-enhancing drugs but are legal. As such, McCarthy believes that athletes should not be singled out for using a drug that will increase their strength and stamina on the playing field. In his view, the ban on performance-enhancing drugs is a result of self-righteous supporters who are quick to judge anything they determine to be a vice. McCarthy concludes that people who criticize drugs in sports are hypocrites because they probably engage in similar behaviors—and thus their argument to ban performance-enhancing drugs does not hold much weight.

Colman McCarthy, "Barry Bonds Is Just Like the Rest of Us," *National Catholic Reporter,* vol. 43, August 31, 2007, p. 18. Copyright © The National Catholic Reporter Publishing Company, 115 E. Armour Blvd., Kansas City, MO 64111. All rights reserved. Reproduced by permission of *National Catholic Reporter,* www.natcath.org.

McCarthy is director of the Center for Teaching Peace in Washington, D.C., and a former columnist for the *Washington Post*. He has written for the *New Yorker, Nation, Progressive, Atlantic Monthly*, and *Reader's Digest* as well as writing biweekly columns for the *National Catholic Reporter*.

AS YOU READ, CONSIDER THE FOLLOWING QUESTIONS:
1. Why has Barry Bonds' home run record been criticized by fans and the media, according to the author?
2. What does the author say is the difference between professional athletes who take drugs and nonathletes who use steroids or other performance-enhancing drugs?
3. According to the author, how does America's war on drugs policy resemble the nationwide ban on alcohol consumption in the 1920s and 1930s?

As if we need still another casualty in the fake and failed war on drugs, Barry Bonds is now under siege. When the champion home-run hitter for the San Francisco Giants cracked his 756th ball into the stands in early August [2007], he dethroned Hank Aaron as the home-run king who 33 years before replaced Babe Ruth. Cheers from hometown fans were matched and often drowned out by sneers and jeers elsewhere. Speculation of the wildest kind condemned Mr. Bonds for steroid use: Performance-enhancing drugs turned a star into a superstar.

FAST FACT

The Anabolic Steroid Control Act of 2004 included sixty drugs in its definition of anabolic steroids.

There Is No Difference Between Athletes Who Use Drugs and Nonathletes Who Do

Corporate media sportswriters scorn Mr. Bonds as a cheater. When told that he has never failed a steroid test, as others have failed, they argue that some steroids are undetectable. When Mr. Bonds himself claims innocence, he is greeted with "Yeah, right, Barry." And, besides, we

In dissenting on a recent Supreme Court decision, Justice John Paul Stevens stated that the war on drugs is reminiscent of the nationwide ban on alcohol consumption when Prohibition was passed.

are told by scribes that Mr. Bonds is arrogant, brusque and therefore unlikable. Translation: He talks back to self-important reporters and sends them packing.

I see steroids and the Bonds case as a personal freedom issue. What's the difference between steroid-using professional athletes risking their health—enlarged heart, cancer, personality disorders—and steroid-using gym rats risking theirs to build bigger bodies? What's the difference between athletes juicing themselves with steroids and drunken fans in the stands doping themselves with the alcohol drug? What's the difference between running up the score with a steroid and scoring with America's favorite performance-enhancer, Viagra?

Performance-Enhancing Drugs Should Not Be Banned
No difference that I can tell, except some drugs are decreed illegal and some legal. The decreers? Prosecutors, legislatures and other moralizers sniffing around with their blue noses and hot to criminalize what they see as vice. Politicians are easily spooked by the issue. When a question came out of left field at a recent presidential candidates' forum on whether he would congratulate Barry Bonds on his achievement, Barack Obama [Democratic Illinois senator and presidential candidate] refused to answer, waffling that he needed more time to think.

While Mr. Obama checks with pollsters and focus groups for a palatable answer, we have the counsel of Justice John Paul Stevens. In the recent 5–4 Supreme Court case that upheld the suspension of an Alaskan high school student for holding a sign—Bong Hits

What Consequences Should Exist for Athletes Who Use Drugs? 67

4 Jesus—during a parade, Justice Stevens in dissenting wrote: "The current dominant opinion supporting the war on drugs in general, and our antimarijuana laws in particular, is reminiscent of the opinion that supported the nationwide ban on alcohol consumption when I was a student. While alcoholic beverages are now regarded as ordinary articles of commerce, their use was then condemned with the same moral fervor that now supports the war on drugs."

"Make All of America Clean" Is an Unrealistic Solution

It was the self-righteous media and Congress that pressured baseball commissioner Bud Selig and the 30 big league team owners to clean up the game. Begin testing.

If that's the agenda, I propose let's really get into it. Full frontal. Make all of America clean. From now on, only unenhanced performances are allowed. Start testing the media, members of Congress and baseball's CEOs. No more reporters turning in caffeine-enhanced copy. No more senators reaching for Jack Daniels after a hard day of cashing checks from lobbyists. No more Viagra for those CEOs pooped after a long session of toting their millions in gate, hot dog and beer receipts.

Any chance of this happening? Don't hold your Breathalyzer.

EVALUATING THE AUTHOR'S ARGUMENTS:

In this viewpoint the author uses rhetorical questions to make his point that it is hypocritical for people to judge athletes who use performance-enhancing drugs. Identify where he uses these questions and explain whether you think they are an effective tool in convincing you of the author's argument.

Chapter 3

How Can Drug Use Among Student Athletes Be Curbed?

A lab technician works with drug test samples of High School athletes. Many states have stopped testing because of possible violations of state laws.

Student Athletes Should Be Drug Tested

Mike Celizic

"If you don't test for steroids, you are telling kids to go ahead and use them, because they won't get caught."

In the following viewpoint Mike Celizic argues that student athletes should be drug tested. Celizic is worried about the nation's student athletes: Since 1991 steroid use has increased 67 percent in high school seniors and shows no sign of slowing. But despite the increased popularity of performance-enhancing drugs in high schools, most teen athletes are not subjected to drug tests. Celizic argues that all other sports associations test their athletes for drugs, including the Olympics, major professional sports leagues, and colleges. Without drug testing, Celizic says, teens are more likely to engage in drug use because they feel they will not be caught. Celizic concludes that making drug testing mandatory in high schools will deter student athletes from using performance-enhancing drugs.

Celizic is a writer based in New York and writes regularly for MSNBC.com.

Mike Celizic, "Time for Steroid Testing in High School; If Kids Can't Get Caught, the Problem Will Only Get Worse," MSNBC.com, April 24, 2004. Republished with permission of MSNBC.com, conveyed through Copyright Clearance Center, Inc.

The question isn't why kids take steroids. Rather, it is why the great majority of teens aspiring to be professional athletes don't take steroids, and why we do virtually nothing to attempt to stop the minority who do.

Steroid Use Among Teen Athletes Has Increased

Statistics vary but the latest national survey of steroid use among teens reports that 3.5 percent of high school seniors admitted to using steroids at least once. That doesn't sound like a lot. But it's a 67 percent increase over the 1991 [survey] and a 17 percent increase over figures cited by the National Institute on Drug Abuse in 1999. So, while the numbers look small, they're rising rapidly, and that's an indictment of an education system that would rather invent reasons why it can't—or won't—do anything about it than find ways to stop it.

Schools Should Test Athletes for Drugs

The Olympics tests for steroids and every other performance-enhancing drug. Pro sports leagues test. Colleges test. High schools, with just a few exceptions, don't test. And if you don't test for steroids, you are telling kids to go ahead and use them, because they won't get caught.

You can lecture kids all you want about the dangers of steroids, about the incredible shrinking testicles and acne blooms and possible liver damage down the road. There are always going to be some, just as there are some athletes at every stage of competition, who are willing to take the risks if they can see a clear reward.

Performance-Enhancing Drugs Are Dangerous

Although some performance-enhancing drugs can make a user faster and bigger, they have physical consequences that can last a lifetime.

Name	Supposed Effect	Medical Research	Medical Risk
Anabolic-androgenic steroids	• Build muscle • Increase strength • Improve performance	• Not proven to improve performance • Increase muscle strength and mass at high doses • Do not increase endurance	• Shrink testicles and cause increased breast tissue in males • Deepen voice, increase facial hair in females • Increase risk of heart attack by increasing blood pressure and cholesterol, possible effect on heart muscle • Liver swelling, jaundice, and tumors • Risk of tendon rupture • Stunted growth in young athletes • "Roid rage"/aggression, addiction, depression • Balding, acne, stretch marks
Androstenedione (Andro), DHEA (dehydroepian-drosterone), "natural steroids"	• Build muscle • Increase strength • Improve performance	• Not proven to build muscle, increase strength, or improve performance • May build muscle at high doses taken frequently	• Same risks as steroids when taken frequently at high levels • Increase female hormone estrogen • Increase certain types of malignant tumors
Ephedra	• Burns fat • Delays fatigue in workouts • Is a stimulant	• Works as stimulant • Effective in "fat burning" when combined with caffeine	• Sudden death • Heart attack • Stroke • Seizures • High blood pressure
Creatine	• Delays fatigue in workouts • Promotes weight gain	• Increases workout capacity for certain weight lifting/sprinting type activity • Increases weight (mainly "water" weight) • Does not increase strength or build muscle • Does not improve endurance (distance events)	• May cause "kidney overload" in certain settings • Dehydration • Muscle cramps • Stomach cramps
Protein supplements	• Promotes weight gain • Build muscle strength /mass	• Do not build muscle strength or mass • Weight gain is variable and dependent on the athlete's routine diet • Also related to calorie and carbohydrate intake	• "Kidney overload" when taken in high concentration

Taken from: American Academy of Pediatrics, November 2004.

Major League Baseball is experiencing a public relations nightmare because, until 2003, it didn't test for any drugs, including steroids. Because it didn't test, players—and no one knows how many—used those drugs as well as human growth hormone to get bigger and stronger. Records fell. Kids watched. And they imitated their heroes.

A recent Associated Press [AP] story on the subject of kids and steroids quoted various high-school officials giving what, for many, is the standard excuse: They can't afford the $50 it costs for each steroid test. For other school systems, including those in New York and New Jersey, civil rights are cited by the few administrators who will even talk on the record about the subject.

But in the same AP report, schools that don't test for steroids do test athletes for other drugs such as marijuana and cocaine. The tests for so-called recreational drugs are relatively inexpensive, but if you're going to test for drugs that don't enhance performance, you're just playing to the bleachers: "Look, we're testing the athletes for drugs." But you're not testing them for the drugs that matter in this regard, the ones that equate with cheating.

Until we do test, the numbers of kids taking the drugs will continue to rise, because the upside of cheating—especially when you can't get caught—is incredible.

Student Athletes Emulate Their Heroes

We celebrate people who are big and strong and fast and skillful, idolize them, buy the products they endorse, dress like them, talk like them, worship the socks they sweat in.

It isn't something we invented, another product of modern decadence. The Greeks idolized athletes and warrior-heroes and were obsessed with physical appearance. Win at the ancient Olympic Games for your city-state and you were set for life, as big a star in that world as athletes are today.

We devote magazines and large sections of our newspapers and television networks and clear-channel radio stations to recording their every move and dissecting their games, talents and lives. And we pay them millions upon millions of dollars so that they live like feudal lords, with the exception that they owe allegiance to no one.

Who wouldn't want a piece of that? What kid with a competitive itch and above-average coordination wouldn't want to get all of that, especially if it involves playing a game in public and being allowed—encouraged even—to spit and scratch without losing social style points.

FAST FACT

The federal government spent $8.6 million on school drug testing programs in 2006.

If you ever played sports as a kid and had any degree of talent you stood in the driveway shooting free throws. You were playing in the Final Four, the national championship game, for State U., 50,000 people screaming in the stands, millions watching on television, a dozen or more of the most beautiful women on campus cheering for you on the sidelines. You were down a point with no time left. Sink both foul shots and your team wins, you're a hero, you get drafted in the NBA lottery, you buy a Hummer and a Porsche and an Escalade and live in a house so big you need a golf cart to get around in it.

Or you spend every quarter you can cadge at the batting cages, and now it's the bottom of the ninth in the World Series. You're playing for the Yankees and you're down three, two outs, bases loaded, the game's greatest relief pitcher on the mound. You take him deep and two weeks later sign a $40-million contract to endorse hamburgers and show up in *People* magazine with a super model on each arm.

Drug Testing Student Athletes Is a Viable Deterrent

As we grow, most of us realize we don't have the talent to reach that dream. But the few who do lock onto it and devote themselves to reaching secular Nirvana. The very few who have surpassing talent have their paths clear. But a lot of kids are on the edge between big-league and also-ran.

Forty years ago, the kids who weren't quite big enough lifted weights to get bigger. Then diet became a big issue and advanced types of training. Eventually, these magic drugs that make your muscles grow like kudzu became popular.

Arnold Schwarzenegger launched a career that has taken him to the California Governor's mansion on steroids. Vince McMahon's pro wrestling empire got where it is via the same vehicle. NFL locker rooms 20 years ago looked like Mr. Universe conventions. Muscles were definitely in.

It's a different world in the NFL today. You don't see the 300-pound guys with 3 percent body fat anymore. You get caught doing steroids, it's a four-game suspension for the first offense. It's not worth it.

But it is worth it in high school, because you can't get caught. The rewards of being one of the few who makes the big time are enormous. When you're talking to kids who feel immortal, dire warnings of what can happen down the line don't cut it.

A urine sample collection kit is used to test for illegal use of drugs in sports. Many high school officials say their schools cannot afford the cost of the drug kits for all their athletes.

Student Athletes Must Be Tested for Drugs

We have to find the national will to test for performance-enhancing drugs at the level at which the greatest numbers compete, at the level at which kids are being told every day that if they get bigger and stronger, they can make it to the next step on the climb to superstardom.

And it can't be left to the individual school systems. When they say they don't have the money, they're not just avoiding the issue; they're being honest. State governments and the federal government, which are bigger on talking about education than actually paying for it, have to find the money to do this.

It's not really an option, something we can do or not do. We want our competition to be clean. That means testing kids in high school. Now.

EVALUATING THE AUTHOR'S ARGUMENTS:

In the viewpoint you just read, Mike Celizic uses history, facts, and examples to make his point that student athletes should be tested for performance-enhancing drugs. He does not, however, use any quotations to support his point. If you were to rewrite this article and insert quotations, what authorities might you quote from? Where would you place these quotations to bolster the points Celizic makes?

Student Athletes Should Not Be Drug Tested

Jennifer Kern, Fatema Gunja, Alexandra Cox, Marsha Rosenbaum, Judith Appel, and Anjuli Verma

"For those who do participate in sports, testing is a poor substitute for learning and appreciating the value of fair play."

In the following viewpoint Jennifer Kern, Fatema Gunja, Alexandra Cox, Marsha Rosenbaum, Judith Appel, and Anjuli Verma argue that drug testing student athletes does not curb drug use among teen sports participants. Although drug testing has been instituted in a number of high schools across the nation, it has not proven to effectively deter students from using performance-enhancing drugs. In fact, the authors argue, student drug testing does more harm than good because it breaks the trust students feel toward school administrators, parents, and coaches. It may even cause some students to quit sports altogether: some may want to avoid testing while others have concerns about privacy and confidentiality. The authors conclude that education and prevention programs are better at decreasing drug use in student athletes and as such are much better alternatives to drug testing.

Jennifer Kern, Fatema Gunja, Alexandra Cox, Marsha Rosenbaum, Judith Appel, and Anjuli Verma, *Making Sense of Student Drug Testing: Why Educators Are Saying No.* New York: American Civil Liberties Union and the Drug Policy Alliance, 2006. Reproduced by permission.

Kern is a research associate at the Drug Policy Alliance's Office of Legal Affairs in Berkeley, California, and serves as the national campaign coordinator for Drug Policy Alliance's "Drug Testing Fails Our Youth" public education project. Gunja is an associate of the American Civil Liberties Union's Drug Policy Litigation Project. Cox is a contributor to *Making Sense of Student Drug Testing*. Rosenbaum is the director of the San Francisco office of the Drug Policy Alliance. Appel is the executive director of San Francisco–based nonprofit Our Family Coalition, a Lesbian Gay Bisexual Transgender family advocacy group. Verma is the public education coordinator for the American Civil Liberties Union Drug Policy Litigation Project.

AS YOU READ, CONSIDER THE FOLLOWING QUESTIONS:
1. What two reasons do the authors give for steroid tests not adequately addressing drug problems?
2. According to the authors, what two comprehensive drug education programs have been more successful than drug testing in decreasing performance-enhancing drug use among students?
3. Since implementing drug testing, what school district has seen a decrease in teen participation in sports, according to the authors?

The use of anabolic steroids and other performance-enhancing supplements by professional athletes has prompted legislators and other policymakers to address steroid use among adolescents. On the surface, random drug testing appears to be a viable, effective deterrent to many. Research, however, does not support this approach. As with other forms of drug testing, those targeting steroids have not proven to be an effective means of reducing use. Further, steroid testing impairs the relationship of trust between students, parents, coaches and other school administrators.

Testing Does Not Adequately Address the Problem
Most steroid tests do not detect other performance-enhancing supplements, and the more substances that are added to a test, the higher the cost. Also, testing does not reach all of those adolescents who are using steroids, as more than one-third of adolescent users do not

participate in school sports. For those who do participate in sports, testing is a poor substitute for learning and appreciating the value of fair play.

Testing Is Too Expensive

The average test ranges from $100 to $200 per test. The New Orleans *Times-Picayune* reported that a local coach estimated steroid tests for his football team would cost $7,000. He commented. "And I have a budget of $9,000. You know what [drug testing] would do to

Many students who want to participate in their school's extracurricular activities may shy away from doing so because of their school's drug testing policies that may make students feel uneasy.

Teenage Steroid Use

This graph shows the percentage of 10th- and 12th-graders who reported using steroids from 2003 through 2007.

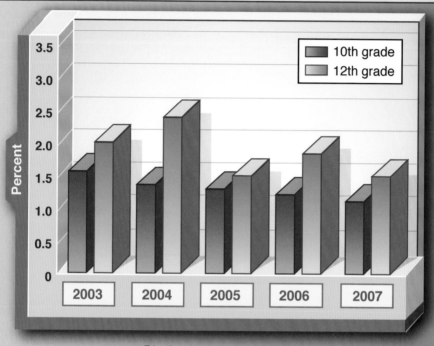

Taken from: National Institute on Drug Abuse.

sports at this school? It would shut us down." As Robert F. Kanaby, Executive Director of the National Federation of State High School Associations, observes, "We must recognize that in an era of scarce resources, steroid testing is way down on [the] budgetary pecking order for most school districts. This is particularly true if there is another good way to address the problem, and there is.

Alternatives to Steroid Testing

Whenever a school considers implementing a testing program, it should first consider education and prevention alternatives, which have a proven track record and reach a broader range of students. These programs also provide students with improved sports nutrition skills, a greater ability to refuse an offer of steroids as well as less desire to engage in future use of steroids. Two effective and proven programs are Athletes Training and Learning to Avoid Steroids (ATLAS) and Athletes Targeting Healthy Exercise and Nutrition Alternatives (ATHENA).

Another approach schools should consider is increased or mandatory coach education about steroids and other performance-enhancing supplements. As a general rule, coaches should neither offer nor encourage the use of any substance having negative or undetermined effects on adolescent health. Coaches, not students, should be the focus of administrative disciplinary actions and be held responsible for sustaining an environment that promotes individual health and the value of fair play.

Random Drug Testing Is a Barrier to Joining Sports

Random drug testing is typically directed at students who want to participate in extracurricular activities, including athletics, which have proven among the most effective pathways to preventing adolescent drug use. However, all too often drug testing policies actually prevent students from engaging in these activities.

Research shows a vastly disproportionate incidence of adolescent drug use and other dangerous behavior occurs during the unsupervised hours between the end of classes and parents' arrival home in the evening.

Research also shows that students who participate in extracurricular activities are:

> **FAST FACT**
>
> The 2007 *Monitoring the Future* study, which surveys drug use in students, found that only 1.5 percent of 8th graders, 1.8 percent of 10th graders, and 2.2 percent of 12th graders have used steroids in their lifetimes.

- Less likely to develop substance abuse problems;
- Less likely to engage in other dangerous behavior such as violent crime; and
- More likely to stay in school, earn higher grades, and set and achieve more ambitious educational goals.

In addition, after-school programs offer students who are experimenting with or misusing drugs productive activities as well as contact with teachers, coaches and peers, who can help them identify and address problematic drug use.

The Tulia Independent School District [in Texas], one of the many districts facing heightened public concerns about privacy and confidentiality, has seen a dramatic reduction in student participation in extracurricular activities since implementing drug testing. One female student explains:

> "I know lots of kids who don't want to get into sports and stuff because they don't want to get drug tested. That's one of the reasons I'm not into any [activity]. Cause . . . I'm on medication, so I would always test positive, and then they would have to ask me about my medication, and I would be embarrassed. And what if I'm on my period? I would be too embarrassed." . . .

Drug Testing Does Not Identify All Drug Users

Drug testing says very little about who is misusing or abusing drugs. Thousands of students might be tested in order to detect a tiny fraction of those who may have used the drugs covered by the test. Additionally, students misusing other harmful substances not detected by drug tests will not be identified. If schools rely on drug testing, they may undervalue better ways of detecting young people who are having problems with drugs. Most often, problematic drug use is discovered by learning to recognize its common symptoms. Properly trained teachers, coaches and other school officials can identify symptoms of a potential drug problem by paying attention to such signs as student absences, erratic behavior, changes in grades and withdrawal from peers.

> **EVALUATING THE AUTHORS' ARGUMENTS:**
>
> In this viewpoint the authors argue that drug testing student athletes causes more harm than good and is an ineffective way to deal with student drug use. The author of the preceding viewpoint, Mike Celizic, says drug tests are the only way to deter students from using performance-enhancing drugs. With which perspective do you agree? Why?

Viewpoint 3

Drug Testing Could Increase Drug Use in Student Athletes

"Requiring drug testing of an entire school population might put some teenagers at risk of serious harmful consequences, and policy makers need to be aware of this."

John R. Knight and Sharon Levy

In the following viewpoint authors John R. Knight and Sharon Levy discuss a scientific study that showed that mandatory drug testing can increase drug use in student athletes. The authors argue that rather than encouraging students to steer clear of drugs, mandatory drug tests encourage them to do drugs that are harder to detect. For example, the authors claim that drug tests encourage users of marijuana (which is readily detected in drug tests) to switch to harder drugs such as inhalants, which are not as easily detected but much worse for them. In addition, drug testing is expensive and sometimes produces erroneous results. A mistake on a drug test could ruin a teen's life, getting them kicked off their team and shunned by their peers. For these reasons, the authors conclude that policy makers and educators must carefully

John R. Knight and Sharon Levy, "The National Debate on Drug Testing in Schools," *Journal of Adolescent Health*, vol. 41, November 2007, pp. 419–420. Republished with permission of Elsevier, conveyed through Copyright Clearance Center, Inc.

consider the negative consequences of imposing mandatory drug tests on students.

John R. Knight is associate director for medical education, Division on Addictions at Harvard Medical School. Sharon Levy is an instructor in pediatrics at Harvard Medical School.

AS YOU READ, CONSIDER THE FOLLOWING QUESTIONS:

1. According to the authors, an argument could be made that schoolwide drug testing amounts to what?
2. What did the American Academy of Pediatrics conclude in 2007 about the safety of drug tests for students?
3. What percent of laboratory drug tests are susceptible to error, as reported by the authors?

This issue of the *Journal of Adolescent Health* includes a report by Linn Goldberg and colleagues on a randomized trial of laboratory testing for drugs of abuse in school. This is a well-designed study that was undoubtedly difficult to carry out. The investigators had to endure a number of legal challenges to the study, and were forced to exclude several schools from their sample as a result. Although scientific study will never settle legal or ethical questions, after all this time and effort, one would hope that the current report would help guide the contentious national debate by either supporting or refuting the efficacy of school-based drug testing.

The Courts Have Legalized Drug Testing

In 1995, the U.S. Supreme Court ruled (*Vernonia v. Acton*) that random drug testing of high school athletes was constitutional and, in June 2002, the Court went further in a 5-to-4 decision and ruled that public schools have the authority to perform random drug tests on all middle and high school students participating in extracurricular activities (*Board of Education v. Earls*). Writing for the majority, Justice Clarence Thomas said, "Testing students who participate in extracurricular activities is a reasonably effective means of addressing the School District's legitimate concerns in preventing, deterring and detecting drug use." It is interesting that the Supreme

Court has not ruled that laboratory testing of all students, including those who do not participate in extracurricular activities, is constitutional. Because school attendance is legally required of all youth, the argument could be made that school-wide drug testing amounts to unreasonable search and seizure. Despite this lack of a definitive court decision, some school districts have implemented universal drug testing policies, and a national debate has arisen on the merits of drug testing for all students in school.

A Bitter Debate over Testing

Shortly after the second Supreme Court ruling, the President's Office of National Drug Control Policy published a guidebook, "What You Need to Know About Drug Testing in Schools," designed to encourage schools to incorporate drug testing for all students. In opposition, the American Civil Liberties Union and the Drug Policy Alliance published a guidebook entitled "Making Sense of Student Drug Testing: Why Educators are Saying No".

In 1996, the American Academy of Pediatrics published a policy statement titled "Testing for Drugs of Abuse in Children and Adolescents," which opposes involuntary testing of adolescents for drugs of abuse. The policy statement takes the position that laboratory testing for drugs under any circumstances is improper unless the patient and clinician can be assured that the test procedure is valid and reliable and patient confidentiality is ensured. In 2007, the American Academy of Pediatrics published an addendum to this policy designed to specifically address drug testing at schools and at home. The addendum reviewed the scant available scientific evidence on the topic and concluded that "drug testing [should] not be implemented before its safety and efficacy are established and adequate substance abuse assessment and treatment services are available". A previous editorial in the *Journal of Adolescent Health* supported the addendum, adding that "drug

> **FAST FACT**
>
> A 2007 study by the Oregon Health and Science University found that the rate of drug use among student athletes at schools with drug testing does not differ from the rate among athletes who are not given such tests.

Dr. Linn Goldberg, a professor of medicine, testifies before Congress about his report on random drug testing in schools published in the Journal of Adolescent Health.

testing may be a valuable adjunct with individual patients, but a more effective approach to screening in the office is the use of validated brief screening instruments to identify at-risk adolescents".

Drug Testing Puts Students at Risk for Hard Drug Use

Although we might hope that the present study by Goldberg would help to end the national debate, this hope is unlikely to be realized on the basis of this report, which includes ample "evidence" to fuel the fire on both sides. Those in favor of student drug testing will point to the significant difference between the testing schools and controls on the endpoint of past-year use, and those opposed will point to the absence of significant between-groups differences at all endpoints for past-month use, the usual standard for measurement of *current* use of alcohol and drugs. In addition, the report finds an increase in important risk factors among students at drug testing schools. Finally, the present Goldberg study was not designed to determine the possible adverse effects and financial burden of random drug testing programs for high school students, and the significance of these costs should be determined prior to implementing large-scale drug testing programs.

In our personal experience of administering a therapeutic drug testing program for adolescents identified with substance abuse problems, we have had patients switch from use of marijuana, which is relatively less harmful but easily detectable in urine, to use of inhalants, which are relatively more harmful but not readily detectable in urine. Other patients have run away from home rather than face the results of a positive drug test. Although these have been unusual events, the consequences have been quite serious, and have demanded intensive clinical work to assure patient safety.

Drug Tests Are Often Wrong

Other risks include the possibility of students facing disciplinary action or other negative consequences on the basis of a *false positive* drug test, or of parents, coaches, and administrators being erroneously reassured that a student is not using drugs because of a *false negative* drug test. We recently published a report demonstrating that greater than 10% of laboratory drug tests performed as part of our adolescent outpatient program were susceptible to error. Requiring drug testing of an entire school population might put some teenagers at risk of serious harmful consequences, and policy makers need to be aware of this possibility.

Finally, this report does not assess the financial cost of drug testing. High-quality drug testing such as the type used in this study is expensive, and resources may be better spent on evidence-based prevention programs or on establishing more drug treatment programs that are developmentally appropriate for adolescents. Less costly approaches to screening, such as confidential interviews of students, might be as effective as laboratory tests in detecting drug use and more effective in identifying high risk drug use.

We Cannot Support Mandatory Drug Tests

In the end, both opponents and proponents of school-based drug testing can all agree that prevention and detection of drug use by adolescents is a national public health priority. The question of how best to accomplish this goal has not yet been determined. The work by Goldberg et al is intriguing in both the information it provides and the questions it raises. Policy makers should be cautious in implementing drug testing programs until more of these questions are answered.

> **EVALUATING THE AUTHORS' ARGUMENTS:**
>
> In this viewpoint the authors suggest that instead of being tested for drugs, students should be screened for drugs via confidential interviews. They claim this method of screening costs less than drug tests and is safer for students. What is your opinion? Would confidential interviews be a better way to reduce drug use among students than mandatory drug tests? Why or why not?

A Comprehensive Education Program Can Reduce Drug Use in Student Athletes

Linn Goldberg

"[Comprehensive education programs] can improve the health of young athletes and recapture the healthy mission of sport."

In the following viewpoint Linn Goldberg argues that performance-enhancing drug use among student athletes can be reduced with comprehensive education programs. Teen athletes are using performance-enhancing drugs at alarming rates in order to be like their favorite athletes who are glamorized by the media. Some teens will do anything to achieve athletic success, including taking performance-enhancing drugs. Goldberg says the best way to curb drug use in student athletes is to develop comprehensive education programs that are taught by clean student athletes and facilitated by trusted coaches. Such programs would be effective, says Goldberg, because teens are more likely to listen to other students than to adults. Furthermore, peer teachers are more likely to tell the truth rather

Linn Goldberg, "Hearing Testimony; Steroids in Sports: Cheating the System and Gambling Your Health," *U.S. House of Representatives; Subcommittee on Commerce, Trade, and Consumer Protection; Committee on Energy and Commerce,* March 10, 2005. Reproduced by permission of the author.

than use scare tactics (which are favored by some antidrug campaigns). Goldberg concludes that developing these programs in high schools across the nation is the best way to combat student athlete drug use.

Linn Goldberg is a practicing physician, professor of medicine, and head of the Division of Health Promotion and Sports Medicine at Oregon Health and Science University. He also serves on the Oregon House of Representatives Speaker's Council on Youth Abuse of Drugs and Alcohol and is the principal investigator of the ATLAS (Adolescents Training and Learning to Avoid Steroids) intervention sponsored by the National Institute on Drug Abuse.

AS YOU READ, CONSIDER THE FOLLOWING QUESTIONS:
1. According to the author, how many high school students have used or were using steroids in 2004?
2. What four components does the author say make an effective performance-enhancing drug prevention program?
3. A comprehensive education program like ATLAS/ATHENA reduces new steroid use in adolescent boys by how much, according to the author?

It is difficult to be a teenage athlete today. More than 50% of high school students participate in school-sponsored athletics, and these student-athletes face the pressure to succeed, perform at a high level, and win for themselves, their team, parents, schools and communities. When winning becomes more important than developing well-adjusted student-athletes, this often translates into substance abuse and antisocial behavior.

Student Athletes Comprise a Large Number of Steroid Users

Anabolic steroid use has invaded the world of adolescent sport. Despite a perception that student-athletes are not involved in unhealthy behaviors, young athletes participate in substance abuse at a rate similar to that of non-athletes and they have even higher rates of performance-enhancing drug and supplement use. The most recent *Monitoring the Future*[1] survey shows that past year and past month steroid use

[1] An ongoing study of the behaviors, attitudes, and values of American students.

among high school seniors is at its highest level since self-reported use was first assessed over a decade ago. The arrest of Utah high school students traveling in a van loaded with steroids, and the recent admitted use of these drugs by high school teams in Arizona and Texas, are reminders that this problem requires immediate action.

Despite the focus on steroid use among selected professional and Olympic athletes, and news reports of use by police officers, the vast majority of steroid users are in our nation's high schools. Based on the May, 2004 Centers for Disease Control report, there are more

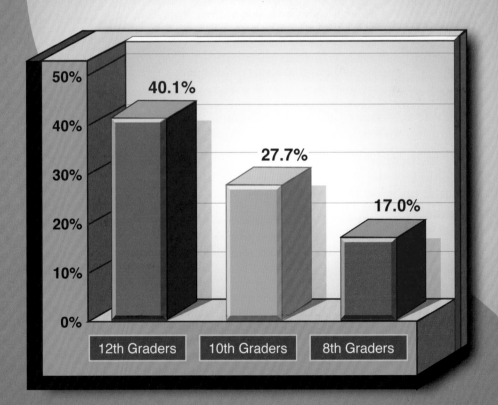

How Easy Is It for Students to Get Steroids?

According to a 2007 *Monitoring the Future* survey, older students have an easier time obtaining steroids than younger students. The following graph shows the percentage of students who said it was "fairly or very" easy to get steroids.

50%

40.1%

40%

27.7%

30%

17.0%

20%

10%

0%

12th Graders   10th Graders   8th Graders

Taken from: National Institute on Drug Abuse.

than 800,000 high school students who have used or are currently using anabolic steroids. Also, because steroids have not been a focus of youth drug prevention, and since high school drug prevention is limited, young athletes are unprotected at a time when they are particularly vulnerable to the inducements and risks of these drugs.

Adolescents Face Many Pressures to Succeed

Steroid use among children and adolescents has several origins. Besides the significant role model effect from high profile steroid abusing athletes, there are gender and media pressures. For adolescent females, the desire toward being thin is compounded by the needs of their sport, resulting in disordered eating, depressive symptoms and use of body-shaping drugs, including steroids. For young male athletes, there are unrealistic expectations for their future as collegiate and professional athletes, coupled with risk-taking and impulsive behaviors that lead to performance-enhancing drug use. Adolescent male steroid use has been found to be related to anti-social behavior, and use of alcohol and other drugs.

Another critical influence toward the acceptance of steroid use may have emerged among advertisers who glibly use the term, "on steroids" to market their products. These strategies promote the idea that being "on steroids" relates to their merchandise being bigger and better. This includes the 3-M corporation's ad stating that its "Post-it Easel" is like a "Post-it Note" on steroids, or U.S. Satellite Broadcasting's boast that its digital picture and sound are like "putting your TV on steroids." A recent shoe ad describes its cross training athletic shoe to be "cross trainers on steroids," while a Saab automobile advertisement compared their vehicle's engine to the large muscles derived from steroid use with the title, "Saab vs Steroids." Could anyone imagine marketing strategy that makes the analogy that their product is "on" any other drug of abuse, like cocaine, LSD, or marijuana? In our society, only steroid drugs are associated with being bigger and better and used in ad campaigns.

Performance-Enhancing Drugs Are Harmful

Anabolic steroid use has numerous risks. These risks may be even greater among adolescents, due to differences in physiology, body mass, and maturity. Current scientific data probably underestimates the actual harmful effects of steroid use because of the low doses studied in most research, which do not approach the typical doses used by steroid users. Because there are no long-term scientific studies of use at the extreme levels taken by athletes, research into the effects have been left to animal studies, case reports, and lower dose use. These documented harms include: 1) increased risk for cardiovascular disease, including heart attacks and strokes; 2) the risk of various liver diseases, especially for those who use the oral steroids; 3) tumors, including those of the prostate and liver; 4) tendon rupture; 5) kidney failure; 6) masculinization of women; 7) stunting the height of children and adolescents; and 8) psychological disturbances ranging from suicidal depression to uncontrolled aggression. In addition, because of needle sharing, the risk of HIV/AIDS, hepatitis, and serious infections are ever-present.

FAST FACT

According to a study published in the February 2006 issue of *Journal of School Health*, female athletes who participate in the ATHENA (Athletes Targeting Healthy Exercise and Nutrition Alternatives) program are less likely to have eating disorders or take diet pills.

Developing an Effective Prevention Program

So, what is the solution? To combat the growing use of steroids and associated behaviors, my colleague Diane Elliot and I engaged in 4 years of formative research. Initially we learned what would not work. We found that scare tactics, informational pamphlets and adult lectures would not deter students from steroid use, since high school students don't enjoy lectures, don't read pamphlets and often feel invulnerable. What we did learn however, was that an effective prevention program would need four major components. First, we needed to separate the girls and boys, because their risk and protective factors for harmful behaviors differ. Second, the information and discussions needed to be led by peers, because kids listen to kids, and the venue should be a place where students work together and share common goals. Third, there needed to be younger and older students present, so the more mature students could serve as role models. Fourth, an instructor needed to

Linn Goldberg, cofounder of the ATLAS and ATHENA Drug Prevention Programs, shakes hands with Washington Redskins kicker Shaun Suisham after the Redskins announced they would join his programs.

be someone the students respect, in and out of the classroom. As you can see, these necessary components are present in every high school sport team.

After learning these lessons, we applied for and were awarded funding from the National Institute on Drug Abuse. With NIDA funding, ATLAS, the program for young men, and ATHENA, the program for young women, were born. ATLAS and ATHENA are team-centered programs, with most of the teaching performed by student athletes, and facilitated by the coach. These programs provide healthy sports nutrition and strength-training as alternatives to use of athletic-enhancing and body-shaping drugs, while reducing risk factors that promote use of alcohol and other illicit substances that can harm sport performance. The messages and activities are clear and tailored to each gender. Not only are these programs successful, kids really enjoy them. Today, schools from 29 states and Puerto Rico have selected these programs for use.

Comprehensive Education Reduces Steroid Use

The results of ATLAS and ATHENA have been published in prestigious, peer-reviewed scientific journals, including *JAMA* (*Journal of the American Medical Association*) and the *Archives of Pediatrics and Adolescent Medicine*. Findings for ATLAS include:

- Significant decreases in alcohol and illicit drug use
- More than 50% reduction in new anabolic steroid use
- More than 40% reduction in performance-enhancing supplement use
- 24% reduction in drinking and driving
- Improved dietary behaviors, increased physical capacity, and reduced body fat

For ATHENA, the changes include:

- More than 50% reduction in new sport supplements, amphetamines & steroid use
- More than 50% reduction in new and ongoing use of diet pills
- Long-term reductions in alcohol and marijuana use
- A reduction in riding in cars with drinking drivers, and an increase in seat belt use
- A reduction in new sexual activity
- Improved nutrition and strength training behaviors
- Fewer sports injuries

Comprehensive Education Must Be Implemented in All School Districts

The high school years represent a critical window of opportunity to prevent the use of steroids, alcohol and other drugs. During this period, students are establishing habits that will last a lifetime. Schools need to do what they do best . . . educate. They need to educate coaches, parents and their athletes. ATLAS and ATHENA are examples of rigorous research initiatives that have turned into important public health interventions that can be easily implemented by school districts throughout the United States. ATLAS and ATHENA and programs modeled after them can improve the health of young athletes and recapture the healthy mission of sport.

EVALUATING THE AUTHOR'S ARGUMENTS:

In the viewpoint you just read, the author suggests that comprehensive education programs taught by student athletes and facilitated by coaches provide the most effective means of reducing performance-enhancing drug use in student athletes. What do you think? Do you agree that students would be more willing to listen to peers than adults? Do you think this is an effective solution? Explain your thoughts.

Facts About Athletes and Drug Use

Editors' note: These facts can be used in reports or papers to reinforce or add credibility when making important points or claims.

History

- According to the National Institute on Drug Abuse (NIDA), anabolic steroids were developed in the late 1930s to treat men with hypogonadism, a condition in which the testes do not produce sufficient amounts of testosterone.
- According to the National Collegiate Athletic Association (NCAA), professional football players began using amphetamines in the 1940s.
- Amphetamines were first synthesized in 1887, according to the NCAA.
- According to the British Broadcasting Corporation (BBC), scientists first isolated the human growth hormone in 1956.
- According to the BBC, the use of synthetic HGH was banned in sports in 1989.

Prevalence

- According to an article in *Sports Illustrated*, 15 million Americans use performance-enhancing drugs.
- The Mayo Clinic reports that 10 percent of steroid users (approximately 300,000 people) are teenagers.
- More than 1 million American adults have taken steroids, according to a survey conducted by the Substance Abuse and Mental Health Services Administration.
- According to the 2007 *Monitoring the Future* study:
  - 1.5 percent of eighth graders, 1.8 percent of tenth graders, and 2.2 percent of twelfth graders have used steroids at least once in their lives.
  - 17 percent of eighth graders, 27.7 percent of tenth graders, and 40.1 percent of twelfth graders report that steroids are easy to obtain.
  - 0.8 percent of eighth graders, 1.1 percent of tenth graders, and 1.4 percent of twelfth graders have used steroids in the past year.
- A survey conducted by the Centers for Disease Control and Prevention (CDC) in 2005 found that nearly 5 percent of high school students have used steroids without a doctor's prescription.

- Steroid use doubled among U.S. high school students between 1991 and 2003, according to a May 2004 report by the CDC.
- According the official Web site of Major League Baseball (www.mlb.com), in 2003 between 5 and 7 percent of players tested positive for drugs. Those positive tests led to mandatory drug testing in the sport.
- According to the Web site Baseball Almanac (www.baseball-almanac.com), twenty-two major league players were suspended for steroid use between the 2005 and 2007 seasons.
- As stated on the NCAA Web site, approximately 1 percent of tests for banned substances have positive results.
- According to the NCAA, 4.1 percent of student athletes used amphetamines in 2005, 2.5 percent used ephedrine, and 1.2 percent took anabolic steroids.

Effects
- According to the NIDA, steroid use can cause the following conditions:
  - heart attacks
  - strokes
  - liver disease
  - cardiovascular disease
  - weakening of the immune system
  - depression
  - mania
  - violent aggression
  - baldness
  - severe acne
- Steroids can remain in a person's body between one week and four months, according to the National Clearinghouse for Alcohol and Drug Information.
- According to the NCAA, the side effects of erythropoietin (EPO) include thickening of the blood and artery blockages.
- The NCAA reports that the consequences of amphetamine use include heat stroke, kidney damage, hallucinations, and paranoid delusions.
- The Office of National Drug Control Policy (ONDCP) reports that people who stop using steroids can suffer withdrawal symptoms including insomnia, depression, and mood swings. These symptoms can last for as long as a year.

- A study published in the *Annals of Internal Medicine* in March 2008 found that use of human growth hormone (HGH) does not improve athletic performance and can cause problems such as carpal tunnel syndrome and joint pain.

Responses

- According to a December 2007 MSN-Zogby poll, 58 percent of American sports fans enjoy watching sports less because the athletes might be taking performance-enhancing drugs.
- According to a spring 2005 poll conducted by the Sacred Heart University Polling Institute, 87 percent of Americans support random testing of high school athletes for steroid use.
- According to an article in *USA Today*, steroid tests cost between $150 and $200.
- According to the ONDCP, drugs can remain present in hair for as long as ninety days.
- An article in the *Los Angeles Times* reports that less than 5 percent of high schools have drug testing programs.
- A 2006 study by the NCAA has found that only 32 percent of college athletes have ever been tested for drug use.
- According to a 2006 study by the NCAA, 59 percent of colleges have a drug testing program.
- A 2006 survey of four hundred school superintendents, published in the American Association of School Administrators newsletter, found that 78 percent of respondents are not interested in implementing mandatory drug tests.
- Per an article in the *Atlanta Journal-Constitution*, the only collegiate athletic conferences that require drug testing are the Big 10 and the Big 12.
- Only 10 to 15 percent of athletes are tested for drugs at major competitions, according to the International Amateur Athletic Federation.
- According to its Web site, the U.S. Anti-Doping Agency (USADA) administered 7,801 drug tests in 2007.
- According to its Web site, in 2004–2005 the NCAA conducted 10,094 tests of student athletes; 49 tested positive for steroids.
- According to a 2005 Gallup poll, 56 percent of baseball fans believe steroid use is a serious problem, and an additional 30 percent believe it is ruining the game.
- A 2005 *USA Today* poll of professional baseball players found that 79 percent believe steroids are at least partly responsible for records set in the sport.

Organizations to Contact

The editors have compiled the following list of organizations concerned with the issues debated in this book. The descriptions are derived from materials provided by the organizations. All have publications or information available for interested readers. The list was compiled on the date of publication of the present volume; the information provided here may change. Be aware that many organizations take several weeks or longer to respond to inquiries, so allow as much time as possible.

Canadian Center for Ethics in Sports (CCES)
350-955 Green Valley Circle
Ottawa, Ontario, K2C 3V4 Canada
(613) 521-3340
fax: (613) 521-3134
e-mail: info@cces.ca
www.cces.ca

CCES is an organization that promotes drug-free sports in Canada and in international competitions. Among its responsibilities is the administration of drug tests in Canadian athletic programs. Materials available on the Web site include educational materials, annual reports, and research papers such as Ethical Challenges and Responsibilities Regarding Supplements.

Drug Enforcement Administration (DEA)
2401 Jefferson Davis Highway
Alexandria, VA 22301
(202) 307-1000
www.dea.gov

The DEA is the federal agency charged with enforcing the nation's drug laws. The agency concentrates on stopping the smuggling and distribution of narcotics in the United States and abroad. It publishes the *Drug Enforcement Magazine* three times a year.

International Amateur Athletic Federation (IAFF)

17 Rue Princesse Florestine
BP 359MC 98007 Monaco Cedex, Monaco
(377) 9310-8888
www.iaaf.org

The IAFF is the international governing body of athletics, with 180 member federations around the world. It produces its own list of doping control regulations and distributes an antidrug booklet for young athletes. Its Web site has a section devoted to antidoping efforts.

International Olympic Committee (IOC)

Chateau de Vidy
CH-1007 Lausanne, Switzerland
fax: 011-41-21-621-6216
www.olympic.org

The IOC oversees the Olympic Games. Its antidoping code prohibits the use of steroids and other performance-enhancing drugs. The Web site provides information on the World Anti-Doping Agency, which was established under the initiative of the IOC, banned substances, and related matters.

National Center for Drug Free Sport

2537 Madison Ave.
Kansas City, MO 64108
(816) 474-8655
fax: (816) 502-9287
e-mail: info@drugfreesport.com
www.drugfreesport.com

The National Center for Drug Free Sport manages most aspects of the National Collegiate Athletic Association's (NCAA) drug testing program. Additional resources provided by the center include the Dietary Supplement Resource Exchange Center and a speakers bureau. The center publishes the quarterly magazine *Insight*.

National Clearinghouse for Alcohol and Drug Information

1 Choke Cherry Rd.
Rockville, MD 20857

(800) 729-6686
http://ncadi.samhsa.gov

The clearinghouse distributes publications of the National Institute on Drug Abuse, the U.S. Department of Health and Human Services, and other federal agencies. Among these publications are *Tips for Teens: The Truth About Steroids* and *NIDA Research Report Series: Anabolic Steroids.*

National Collegiate Athletic Association (NCAA)
700 W. Washington St., PO Box 6222
Indianapolis, IN 46206-6222
(317) 917-6222
fax: (317) 917-6888
e-mail: pmr@ncaa.org
www.ncaa.org

The NCAA oversees intercollegiate athletic programs and provides drug education and drug testing programs in partnership with the National Center for Drug Free Sport. Articles on steroids are frequently published in the NCAA's twice-monthly online newsletter *NCAA News.*

National Strength and Conditioning Association
1885 Bob Johnson Dr.
Colorado Springs, CO 80906
(719) 632-6722
fax: (719) 632-6367
e-mail: nsca@nsca-lift.org
www.nsca-lift.org

Consisting of professionals from the sport science, athletic, health, and fitness industries, the goal of the association is to facilitate an exchange of ideas related to strength training and conditioning practices. It offers career certifications, educational texts and videos, and several publications, including the bimonthly journal *Strength and Conditioning,* the quarterly *Journal of Strength and Conditioning Research,* the monthly Web-based publication *NSCA Performance Training Journal,* and the bimonthly newsletter *NSCA Bulletin.* Papers and position statements are available on the Web site.

United States Anti-Doping Agency (USADA)
2550 Tenderfoot Hill St., Suite 200
Colorado Springs, CO 80906-7346
(866) 601-2632
fax: (719) 785-2001
e-mail: webmaster@usantidoping.org
www.usantidoping.org

The USADA manages the drug testing of U.S. Olympic, Pan Am Games, and Paralympic athletes and enforces sanctions against athletes who take banned substances. The agency also teaches athletes about the risks and ethics of steroid abuse. USADA issues annual reports and the quarterly newsletter *True Sports.*

United States Olympic Committee (USOC)
One Olympic Plaza
Colorado Springs, CO 80909
(719) 632-5551
e-mail: media@usoc.org
www.usoc.org

The USOC is a nonprofit private organization that coordinates all Olympic-related activity in the United States. It works with the International Olympic Committee and other organizations to discourage the use of steroids and other drugs in sports. Information on USOC programs can found on the Web site.

World Anti-Doping Agency (WADA)
800 Place Victoria, Suite 1700, PO Box 120
Montreal QC H4Z 1B7 Canada
(514) 904-92329
fax: (514) 904-8650
e-mail: info@wada-ama.org
www.wada-ama.org

The WADA is an independent international antidoping agency that works with governments, athletes, international sports federations, and national and international Olympic committees to coordinate a comprehensive drug testing program. Its publications include annual reports, the magazine *Play True,* and the newsletter *Athlete Passport.* Information on banned substances and drug testing laboratories is provided on the Web site.

For Further Reading

Books

Aretha, David. *Steroids and Other Performance-Enhancing Drugs.* Berkeley Heights, NJ: MyReportLinks.com Books, 2005. The author details the dangers caused by steroid use, in particular the violent effects of "roid rage."

Carroll, Will. *The Juice: The Real Story of Baseball's Drug Problems.* Chicago: Ivan R. Dee, 2005. This book, which also includes contributions from other authors, looks at performance-enhancing drugs both within the world of sports and as a serious social issue.

Ezra, David. *Asterisk: Home Runs, Steroids, and the Rush to Judgment.* Chicago, IL: Triumph, 2008. The author offers a defense of Barry Bonds, who has been accused of using steroids.

Fainaru-Wada, Mark, and Lance Williams. *Game of Shadows: Barry Bonds, BALCO, and the Steroids Scandal That Rocked Professional Sports.* New York: Gotham, 2006. Two reporters provide an in-depth look at the BALCO steroids scandal and how the drug affected baseball.

Fitzhugh, Karla. *Steroids.* Chicago: Heinemann Library, 2005. This book features a variety of viewpoints on steroids.

Hoberman, John. *Testosterone Dreams: Rejuvenation, Aphrodisia, and Doping.* Berkeley: University of California Press, 2005. The author looks at the role testosterone has played since the 1930s, including its use among athletes.

Jendrick, Nathan. *Dunks, Doubles, Doping: How Steroids Are Killing American Athletics.* Guilford, CT: Lyons, 2006. The author interviews athletes, physicians, and experts on steroid law.

Levert, Suzanne. *The Facts About Steroids.* Tarrytown, NY: Benchmark, 2005. This book looks at the effects and health risks of steroids.

McCloskey, John, and Julian Bailes. *When Winning Costs Too Much: Steroids, Supplements, and Scandal in Today's Sports World.* Lanham, MD: Taylor Trade, 2005. The authors explore the dangers of performance-enhancing drugs and how the modern world of sports emphasizes a win-at-all-costs mentality.

Monroe, Judy. *Steroids, Sports, and Body Image: The Risks of Performance-Enhancing Drugs.* Berkeley Heights, NJ: Enslow, 2004. This book provides information on how steroids work, why people use them, the consequences of steroid use, and alternatives to steroids.

Mottram, David R., ed. *Drugs in Sport.* London: Routledge, 2005. The contributors to this book analyze topics such as steroids, human growth hormone, and nutritional supplements.

Periodicals

Adams, Jacqueline. "The Incredible Bulk," *Science World,* March 28, 2005.

Adler, Jerry. "Toxic Strength," *Newsweek,* December 20, 2004.

Barrett, Wayne M. "Why the Incredible Hulk Is Batting Cleanup," *USA Today Magazine,* May 2004.

Cook, Glenn. "Shortcut to Tragedy," *American School Board Journal,* August 2004.

Duffy, Brian. "Why Cutting Corners Comes as No Surprise," *U.S. News & World Report,* August 7, 2006.

Economist. "Drugs and the Olympics," August 7, 2004.

Hochstetler, Douglas R. ". . . and Sport Shouldn't Be About Who Cheats Best," *Morning Call* (Allentown, PA), October 18, 2007.

Hooton, Donald M. oral testimony, House Government Reform Committee, March 17, 2005. http://republicans.oversight.house.gov/Steroids/2005_03_17_MLB_Steroids/20050317FC_Testimony_Hooten.pdf.

Jenkins, Sally. "Where Athletes Are Concerned, the Wrong Message Is Sent," *Los Angeles Times,* March 9, 2008.

Kayser, Bengt, Alexandre Mauron, and Andy Miah. "Legalisation of Performance-Enhancing Drugs," *Lancet,* December 17, 2005.

Kluger, Jeffrey. "The Steroid Detective," *Time,* March 1, 2004.

Le Page, Michael. "Only Drugs Can Stop the Sports Cheats," *New Scientist,* August 19, 2006.

McCallum, Jack. "The Real Dope: It's Not Just Sports," *Sports Illustrated,* March 17, 2008.

Miller, Sara B. "Steps Toward More Drug Testing in School," *Christian Science Monitor,* May 20, 2005.

Mitten, Matthew J. "Is Drug Testing of Athletes Necessary?" *USA Today Magazine*, November 2005.

Moore, Gregory. "Steroid Test at High School Level a Much Needed Tool," *American Chronicle*, May 29, 2007. www.americanchronicle.com/articles/viewArticle.asp?articleID=28288.

Nature. "A Sporting Chance," August 2, 2007.

Oakland Tribune, "Legal Steroids the Solution," December 15, 2007.

Poniewozik, James. "This Is Your Nation on Steroids," *Time*, December 20, 2004.

Roan, Shari. "Put to the Test," *Los Angeles Times*, May 21, 2007.

Shapin, Steven. "Cleanup Hitters," *New Yorker*, April 18, 2005.

Vecsey, George. "Scamming for Dollars: It's Time to Get Angry About Athletes Who Cheat," *International Herald Tribune*, October 8, 2007.

Verducci, Tom. "Is This the Asterisk Era?" *Sports Illustrated*, March 15, 2004.

Weekly Reader. "Steroids Are the Rage," January 16, 2004.

Wharton, David. "Voice of Dissent in Drug Wars," *Los Angeles Times*, May 9, 2004.

Zedalis, Joe. "Steroid Testing Hits Home at High Schools," Rivals.com, 2008. http://highschool.rivals.com/content.asp?CID=741122.

Web Sites

Baseball's Steroid Era (www.baseballssteroidera.com). This Web site provides information on baseball players who have tested positive; facts about performance-enhancing drugs; and links to articles, interview transcripts, and other documents.

Drug Information: Performance Enhancing Drugs/Steroids (www.drugstory.org/drug_info/performance.asp). Sponsored by the Office of National Drug Control Policy, this site provides information on the mental and physical effects of steroids and links to relevant Web sites.

MedLine Plus: Anabolic Steroids (www.nlm.nih.gov/medlineplus/abolicsteroids.html). Produced by the National Library of Medicine, this Web site provides information on the health risks of steroids and the use of steroids by teenagers and offers links to drug enforcement and anti-drug-abuse organizations.

National Institute on Drug Abuse: Steroid Abuse Web Site (www. steroidabuse.org). A public education initiative of the National Institute on Drug Abuse (NIDA) and several partners, including the American College of Sports Medicine, the American Academy of Pediatrics, and the National College Athletic Association, this Web site provides information and articles that alert people, especially teenagers, about the dangers of anabolic steroids.

Steroid Law (www.steroidlaw.com). Run by criminal attorney and former bodybuilder Rick Collins, who believes that the health risks of steroids have been exaggerated, this Web site provides health and legal information to people curious about using steroids and advocates the reform of current steroid laws.

Index

A

Aaron, Hank, 59, 65

Accomplishment, shortcuts to, 44–45

Adolescents. *See* Teenagers

Allen, Mel, 59

American Academy of Pediatrics, 85

Amphetamines, 7, 8, 50, 60

Anabolic Steroid Control Act, 65

Anabolic steroids. *See* Steroids

Anderson, Greg, 20

Antidoping policies
  are misguided, 54–57
  in baseball, 29–30, 49–52, 61–62
  in professional sports, 49–62
  in USA Track and Field, 60–61
  See also Drug testing

Appel, Judith, 77

Armstrong, Jack, 25

Ashcroft, John, 20

ATHENA (Athletes Targeting Healthy Exercise and Nutrition Alternatives), 7, 8, 81, 93–96

Athletes
  banning of, who test positive, 13–14

cheating by, with steroid use, 37–41

female, 7–9

penalties on, are hypocritical, 64

pressure on, 8, 12–13, 92

records deletion for, 58–63

should be penalized for drug use, 48–52

should not be penalized for drug use, 53–57

See also Olympic athletes; Professional athletes; Student athletes

ATLAS (Athletes Training and Learning to Avoid Steroids), 7, 81, 94–96

B

Bakalar, James B., 46

Baseball
  antidoping policy in, 29–30, 49–52, 61–62
  doping scandal in, 21
  performance-enhancing drugs harm integrity of, 25–31
  performance-enhancing drugs improve, 32–36
  public relations issues in, 73

zero tolerance policy in,
60–62
Sports fans
enjoyment of, is unaffected by
steroid use, 45
opinions of, 13, 14
Sports records, deletion of,
58–63
Steroid use
among teenagers, 7, 60, 71,
80, 90–92
consequences of, 40–41
decline in, 28, 55
education about, 95–96
global, 41
is cheating, 37–41
is not cheating, 42–46
by professional athletes,
25–31, 33–36, 39
public opinion on, 62
by women, 7–8
Steroids
addiction to, 16
dangers of, are exaggerated,
43–44
ease of obtaining, 91
penalties for trafficking in, 19
purpose of, 14
should be allowed, 45
side effects of, 8, 15–16, 26,
60, 72, 92–93
unfairness of, 28–29
Stevens, John Paul, 67–68
Student athletes
education programs for,
89–96

emulation of professional
athletes by, 73–74
increased drug use in, and
drug testing, 83–88
should be drug tested, 70–76
should not be drug tested,
77–82
steroid use by, 90–92
See also Teenagers
Sullum, Jacob, 42
Suspensions, 13–14

T
Talent, 44–45
Teenagers
pressures on, 92
risks to, 26, 28
side effects in, 16, 28
steroid use by, 7, 60, 71, 80,
90–92
See also Student athletes
Testosterone, 20
Thomas, Clarence, 84
Tygart, Travis, 40

U
Ullrich, Jan, 41
U.S. Anti-Doping Agency
(USADA), 20
USA Track and Field
Convention, 59, 60

V
Valente, James, 20

Picture Credits

Maury Aaseng, 13, 20-21, 27, 39, 51, 55, 62, 72, 80, 91

AP Images, 10, 22, 34, 40, 44, 47, 50, 56, 69, 75, 79, 94

© Bob Jones Photography/Alamy, 15

Copyright 2007 by John Cole and CagleCartoons.com. All rights reserved, 36

Copyright 2008 by John Cole and CagleCartoons.com. All rights reserved, 67

Robert Galbraith/Reuters/Landov, 61

Kamenko Pajic/UPI/Landov, 86

Brendan Smialowski/AFP/Getty Images, 66

Chip Somodevilla/Getty Images, 30

About the Editors

Jennifer L. Skancke lives and works in San Francisco. Aside from writing, she loves reading, HBO programming, learning Italian, hiking, camping, traveling, and laughing with friends.

Lauri S. Friedman earned her bachelor's degree in religion and political science from Vassar College in 1999. Her studies there focused on political Islam, and she produced a thesis on the Islamic Revolution in Iran titled *Neither West, Nor East, but Islam.* She also holds a preparatory degree in flute performance from the Manhattan School of Music.

She is the founder of LSF Editorial, a writing and editing outfit in San Diego, CA. Her clients include Greenhaven Press, for whom she has edited numerous titles on gay marriage, drug abuse, the war on terror, Iraq, pandemics, genetic engineering, and more. A former in-house senior editor at Greenhaven, she helped conceive of and design the *Introducing Issues with Opposing Viewpoints* series.

Friedman lives in Ocean Beach, San Diego, with her husband, Randy, and their yellow lab, Trucker. In her spare time she enjoys pottery, making music, taking Trucker to the beach, and traveling.